About the Book

Superstitious country folk thought that the foxglove was created to protect foxes. Anemones were sent to a lover to say "I'm waiting for you" in the once-popular language of flowers. The rose was a staple of ancient medicine. Tulip bulbs were traded for exorbitant sums—before the market "crashed."

These are just a few of the fascinating stories and superstitions that unfold as Peter Limburg tells how more than fifty types of cultivated flowers were named. With an engaging mixture of knowledge and humor the author discusses times when flowers were used widely as home remedies, food, religious symbols, and the special language of lovers. Mr. Limburg brings many interesting insights into the social mores of the past to this study of words. Heidi Palmer's lovely illustrations will add to the reader's enjoyment.

What's in the Names of
Flowers

by Peter Limburg

illustrated by Heidi Palmer

Coward, McCann & Geoghegan, Inc.   New York

SBN: GB-698-30537-X

SBN: TR-698-20285-6

Library of Congress Catalog Card Number: 73-88535

PRINTED IN THE UNITED STATES OF AMERICA

10 up

Designed by Cathy Altholz

What's in the Names of
Flowers

Flower

No one knows how long man has loved flowers. Romans, Greeks, Babylonians, Hindus, and ancient Chinese all appreciated flowers and put them into their legends, art, and religion. In fact, the love of flowers goes back far beyond the earliest civilizations. In a mountain cave in Iraq, archeologists dug up the crude grave of a Neanderthal man. In the grave they found flower pollen. It is almost certain that the survivors of his band buried the flowers with him when he died—more than 60,000 years ago!

From gathering flowers growing wild in forests and meadows, the next step is raising them in gardens, and man has been raising flowers for thousands of years. Flowers have been used in sorcerers' spells and religious ceremonies.

They have played a part in hundreds of myths and folktales. They have inspired poems and paintings. Flowers have been used for medicine, perfume, decoration, and even food. But the real purpose of flowers is to produce seeds to keep their kind of plant going.

The business parts of flowers are the organs that produce the male and female cells that unite to form seeds. In many kinds of flowers the male and female cells are produced by the same plant. The female cells are produced in an organ called the pistil, from the Latin *pistillum*, meaning "pestle." (A pestle is a heavy, clublike implement once used to grind grain and other things in a heavy bowl called a mortar.) The pistil of a flower looks very much like a pestle, hence the name. The pistil has three main parts: the ovary, which contains the female cells (from Latin *ovum*, meaning "egg"); a long tube called the style (from the Latin word for "stake" or "pole"), which sticks up out of the top of the ovary; and a feathery structure called a stigma at the top of the style (from the Greek *stigma*, meaning "mark" or "brand"). The stigma's job is to catch the male cells, or pollen, so that they can fertilize the egg cells down in the ovary.

The pollen (from the Latin *pollen*, meaning "fine flour") is a mass of tiny grains, usually golden yellow in color. It is produced by organs called anthers (from the Greek *anthos*, meaning "flower"), which are borne on the ends of stalks called stamens (a Latin weaver's term from an ancient Indo-European root meaning "to stand").

In our common garden flowers, and in most of our farm crops, the stamens grow in a ring around the pistil. However, some plants have separate male and female flowers.

8

Oak trees and cucumbers are two examples. In some species of plants there are separate male and female plants. The holly tree is one such plant. A female holly cannot produce its bright red berries unless there is a male holly tree nearby.

Fossils many millions of years old give clues that flowering plants evolved from a plant like a pine tree. This primitive plant had separate male and female parts. The male parts probably looked like furry little candles. When they were ripe, they released clouds of pollen that drifted on the wind to the female parts, which were fleshy cones. This system is still used by cone-bearing trees such as pines and spruces. It works well enough when the wind is right, but if the wind is blowing the wrong way, or if there is no wind, the result is few seeds or none at all.

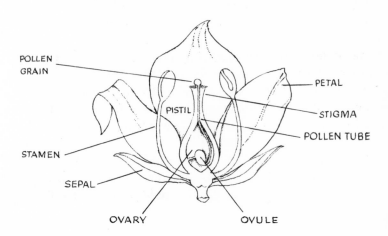

Scientists believe that as insects gradually evolved, some of them learned to feed on the pollen and the seed cones of the primitive pinelike trees. As they flew and crawled from plant to plant, some of the sticky pollen adhered to their bodies and was rubbed off on the seed cones, fertilizing them. However, this was still a pretty haphazard method, and sometimes the insects must have eaten up the seed cones entirely (as happens today), leaving nothing to produce seeds.

In time, some plants developed female organs with their reproductive cells hidden way down inside, instead of vulnerably exposed on the surface. The female parts were surrounded by big, showy leaves like flower petals. These were the first true flowers.

Scientists think that the first flowering plants were pollinated by beetles, which are not very good fliers. The big, showy petals gave the beetles a big target to aim at and also a landing stage that was roomy enough for them not to fall off. As other types of insects evolved, such as butterflies and bees, flowers became adapted to them. Now, after millions of years of evolution, many flowers are so adapted to particular insects that they cannot reproduce without them. Red clover is pollinated by the bumblebee; other insects cannot reach down inside its deep, narrow flower tubes. A certain kind of yucca that grows in the American southwest can only be pollinated by one species of moth. Some flowers have become specialized for being pollinated by birds and bats.

Many flowers are compound flowers, that is, what looks to us like a single flower is actually made up of many small flowers growing together in one flower head. Dandelions and clover have this kind of flower. Daisies and their relatives have another kind of compound arrangement. The yellow circle in the center of the flower is actually made up of hundreds of tiny flowers called florets, each of which can produce a seed. The petals around the edge are specialized, sterile flowers that cannot produce seeds.

The flowers we raise in gardens and florists' greenhouses are specially bred for their blossoms. Some of them are so different from their wild ancestors that only a trained botanist could see their relationship. By playing tricks with light and temperature, man can make flowers bloom at any season. Flower breeders are continually creating new varieties of flowers. But these marvels are possible only because men have learned how to use natural laws. And the spectacular flowers we know today are just one part of the story of nature's evolution.

The word "flower" itself came into the English language in the Middle Ages, some time after the Norman conquest of England. The Normans were the descendants of Viking pirates from Denmark who had settled in France. By the time they conquered England, in 1066, they had forgotten their Danish and spoke French instead. One of the French words they brought to England was *flour* (rhyming with *tour*), the Old French word for "flower." This in turn came from the Latin word *flos, floris*. Until the Norman Conquest, English speakers had used the native Anglo-Saxon words *bloom* or *blossom*, but the word used by the tough, overbearing conquerors gradually pushed the words of the beaten Anglo-Saxons aside and became the commonly used name.

"Flower" early took on the meaning of something especially fine or beautiful. The *flour* from which bread is made was originally the flower, or finest part, of the ground-up grain. When warfare was still very much a matter of single matches between champions, people spoke of the "flower of the knights" of the king of France or some other ruler, meaning his top-ranking knights. Later, if someone of promise died young, it was said that he died in the "flower of his youth." And a song written in the 1890's—and still popular —had as its punch line: "You're the flower of my heart, Sweet Adeline!"

Alyssum

got its name from the ancient Greeks, who used it as a remedy for insanity and the bites of rabid dogs. Its Greek name was *alysson*, from *a* ("not") plus *lyssa* ("madness"). Other peoples must have copied the Greek "cure," for the old English name for the plant was "madwort."

Alyssum was believed to have magical qualities—perhaps that is why people thought it could cure rabies—and witches used it in their eerie and sinister pharmacopoeias of materials for casting spells. Fortunately no one tries to cure rabies with it any longer, or the death rate would rise, magical powers or no.

But with all the magic attached to alyssum, its history is still confusing, for the name has been used for three completely unrelated plants. The original Greek alyssum belonged to the madder family (madder is a prickly plant that was formerly used for red and brown dyes). Later the name was applied to a plant of the mint family. Last of all, about the time of Queen Elizabeth I of England (late 1500's), it was used for a member of the mustard family. This is the plant that gardeners today known as alyssum and grow for its bright yellow flowers.

A related flower is sweet alyssum, a low, creeping plant covered with tiny, fragrant blossoms. The most popular kinds of sweet alyssum are white, but there are also purple and pink varieties.

Flowers have had great symbolical importance in the past. They have been sacred to the gods and goddesses of many religions, and to the Virgin Mary in Christianity. People have also attributed such virtues and vices and emotions to flowers as courage, loyalty, jealousy, sorrow, and love. In the 1800's writers, particularly in England and France, let their imaginations run wild and developed such earlier notions into a whole language of flowers. This was actually a kind of signal code in which each flower stood for a meaning. Thus, a young man might send a girl an alyssum bouquet to say that in his eyes she had worth beyond beauty. Or he might send yellow tulips to tell her that he was hopelessly in love with her. If she liked him, she might respond with a bouquet of China asters to say, "Your sentiments meet with a return." If she were not so sure about it, she might send him daisies to say, "I'll think it over." She might add other flowers indicating where and when he could meet her. (Of course, if the man and the lady of his heart used different books of flower language, some dreadful misunderstandings might result.) This sentimental flower language began to die out after 1900, and today it is virtually unknown.

Amaryllis

More than 2,000 years ago, ancient Greek poets wrote odes to Amaryllis, an imaginary country girl who was loved by an imaginary shepherd. To the Greeks, shepherds and shepherdesses symbolized a virtuous, simple way of life in the country, whose praises they never tired of singing. The poets themselves, however, preferred to live in the wicked cities, Athens and Corinth, where the action was.

The Greeks, at any rate, started a long tradition of pastoral poetry (so called from *pastor*, the Latin word for "shepherd"), which lasted far longer than the Greek civilization. In fact, people are still writing pastoral poetry today. Some of the best pastoral poetry was written about the time of Shakespeare (late 1500's and early 1600's). Shakespeare himself sometimes had his characters recite this kind of poetry. Another famous poet, John Milton, who lived about half a century later than Shakespeare, created the line: "To sport with Amaryllis in the shade." It was a minor line in a

16

long poem called *Lycidas*, in which the poet lamented the death of a young friend, but later poets and writers fell in love with the line and used it until it almost lost its meaning. But it did keep the name of Amaryllis alive until it was given to a flower that the ancient Greeks never knew, for it came from South America.

The amaryllis is a flower that resembles a giant lily, although it does not belong to the lily family, and it was unknown to Europeans until the 1700's. With spectacular, bright-colored flowers measuring as much as six inches across, it hardly suggests a simple shepherdess. Perhaps Linnaeus, the Swedish botanist who christened it, wanted a name that sounded classical and high-toned. At any rate, amaryllises have been popular potted plants for more than 200 years.

Linnaeus was the founder of the modern system of plant classification; he named thousands of plants, and his pupils named even more. His family name was formerly Linné, but

Linnaeus

one of his ancestors tacked a Latin ending onto the name when he became a minister of the state church. Earlier still, the name was probably Lind, meaning "linden tree."

For a time, botanists tried to change the name of amaryllis to *Hippeastrum*, meaning "horse star," because of the size and shape of its flowers. But gardeners and flower lovers kept on calling it amaryllis, and in the end the learned experts gave up.

Anemone

Indians of the Rocky Mountains saw wild anemones swaying and dancing in the breeze and called them "flower of the wind." The ancient Greeks, too, connected anemones with the wind. They believed that they only blossomed when the wind was blowing, and so they named them "daughter of the wind," *anemone* (from *anemos*, "wind").

Anemones belong to the buttercup family. They are native to Europe, Asia, and North America. There is tremendous diversity among wild anemones. Some species are only a couple of inches tall, while others reach nearly waist-high (higher on a short person). The blossoms range from the size of a nickel to the size of a silver dollar, and the colors vary between white, blue, lavender, pink, and red. Different species bloom at different seasons of the year, so that by choosing them carefully, you could have anemones flowering from early spring to late fall.

Although anemones are best known as wildflowers, they have been cultivated since ancient times. The height of their popularity as garden flowers came in the seventeenth and eighteenth centuries, and flower fanciers were sometimes neurotically jealous of their rare varieties. The story is told that one Frenchman, consumed by the wish to have an only-one-of-its-kind collection of exotic Oriental anemones, for years refused to sell plants or seeds from his collection. But he was finally outwitted by a wily government official who "accidentally" dropped his cloak on a bed of anemones that had finished blooming and gone to seed. The visitor's servant, carefully drilled in his part, rushed forward to retrieve the cloak, which had now picked up lots of seeds, and with many apologies hurried home with it to brush it clean. From the seeds that were recovered, the rascally official raised enough plants to fill his own garden and supply all his friends. Eventually the closely guarded anemones were spread all over Europe.

Unlike many of the flowers described in this book, anemones were seldom used in medicine. In fact, they had very few uses, although in medieval times the English used one species to dye Easter eggs bright green.

In the language of flowers, anemones could stand for expectation ("I'm waiting for you!"), forsaken ("Why don't you ever come to see me any more?"), or frailty ("You are a delicate little flower, but I'll take care of you, if you'll only let me"). The message was no doubt clearer if the sender and the recipient of the flowers used the same floral code book.

Aster

The aster is closely related to the chrysanthemum and the daisy. Some of its other relatives are the dahlia, the zinnia, and the marigold. It is also related to the goldenrod, the dandelion, the black-eyed Susan, and all the varieties of the garden lettuce.

Botanists estimate that there are about 600 species of asters, and most of them are native to North America. Some grow in Europe, however, and it was one of these that the Greeks named *aster*, or "star," from the starlike petals of the flowers.

(The same Greek word, *aster*, has also given us "astronomy," literally the arrangement of the stars; "astrology," literally the discussion of the stars; "asterisk," the little star on a printed page that calls attention to a footnote, and "aster-oid," literally a starlike body. And of course, the recently invented word "astronaut.")

The Romans originally called the aster *amellus*, from the river Amella in northern Italy, where they grew in huge numbers, but eventually they took over the Greek name, and centuries later classically trained botanists spread it into every European language.

The Romans thought highly of the aster, although they did not cultivate it. According to the poet Virgil, they often made wreaths of wild purple asters to decorate the altars of their gods. Virgil also wrote that the roots of the aster, boiled in fragrant wine, make an excellent medicine for reviving sick bees. Virgil, who was an enthusiastic farmer as well as an outstanding poet, had such faith in this cure that he recommended serving it in basketfuls at the entrance to the beehive. There was also a folk belief that the smell of burning aster leaves would drive away mice and serpents.

Although the aster may have been good for bees, it was not used to cure the ailments of human beings, at any rate, not in Europe. But some of the Indians of the United States boiled the roots of the dwarf purple aster for a diarrhea remedy, and from the flowers and stems they made a lotion for rheumatism. They boiled and ate the leaves of many species of wild aster, probably when the plants were young and tender—aster leaves get quite rough and hairy as the plants mature, and they would not be very palatable then.

Most wild asters are purple or bluish, but there are also species with white and pink flowers. The golden aster belongs to a related but separate genus. The China aster belongs to another related genus; its botanical name is *Callistephus*, which comes from the Greek for "beautiful crown."

The name "aster" came into the English language around 1600, when the Italian aster (the same one Virgil described) was first imported into England. An old English name, used for a native British aster, was "starwort"—evidently the Greeks were not the only ones who thought the asters looked like stars. Since the Italian aster bloomed around the date of Michaelmas (Saint Michael's day, September 29), it soon acquired the name of Michaelmas daisy. Many people still prefer this name.

Many of the most popular garden varieties of asters are descendants of two wild American asters, the blue-violet New York aster and the deep purple New England aster. Man's selection has produced many colors not found in nature, but they are asters nevertheless.

In the language of flowers, the aster could mean "afterthought," "elegance," "daintiness," and "beauty in retirement," a strange symbolism for such a brilliant flower.

Baby's Breath

is a flower of delicate beauty, with its clouds of tiny white or pink flowers. It is used in huge quantities to create a misty effect in bouquets. It is also a very popular plant for garden borders because it is easy to grow.

Baby's breath belongs to the pink family, along with carnations. Its scientific name, *gypsophila*, means "lime-loving," for the plant grows best in limy soils. It comes from the Greek *gypsos*, "gypsum" (a form of lime), and *philein*, "to love."

"Baby" is a diminutive, pet-name form of "babe." Both words go back to the 1300's, and language experts believe that they come from some older word that imitated the babbling sounds of an infant. "Mama" and "Papa" probably originated the same way.

"Breath" comes from the Anglo-Saxon *braeth* and has been traced back to an ancient Indo-European root, *bhre*, meaning "to burn." Originally it meant the smoke or vapor given off by heated objects; later it came to mean their odor as well. In the Middle Ages, probably around 1300, it took on its present meaning.

Baby's breath must have been named during the Victorian era, which was surely the most sentimental period the Western world ever passed through. Queen Victoria reigned from 1837 to 1901. Her influence extended far beyond the borders of her own British Empire and lingered on for years after her death. The queen did not invent Victorianism and force it on a trembling world, for it was really the spirit of the times in which she lived. But she expressed that spirit so well that she was given credit for it. The Victorian spirit was composed of extreme respectability, publicly displayed piety, a fierce prudery, and other burdensome qualities, all wrapped in a sticky coating of sentimentality. To the untiringly sentimental Victorian mind, what could suggest delicacy and purity better than the breath of an innocent baby, as yet uncorrupted by the wicked world?

Bachelor's Button

At one time, fashionable young men-about-town sported flowers in their buttonholes. From this custom the flowers they wore received the name of "bachelor's button."

"Bachelor" now means an unmarried man, but its ancestry goes back to one of the Latin words for "cow," *vacca*. In some of the Latin dialects that were spoken during the last days of the Roman Empire, *vacca* turned into *bacca*. The farmhand who looked after the cows was called a *baccalarius*. Since this was the sort of job usually given to young men, *baccalarius* may have come to mean simply a young man, and then, by another jump in meaning, a young man in some sort of training. At any rate, the word surfaced in the early Middle Ages as the French *bachelier*, meaning a young knight in training. The scholars at medieval universities were also called "bachelors" when they had completed their first set of courses, which qualified them to study for the master's degree. Neither young trainees for knighthood nor students were cutomarily married, and late in the Middle Ages, probably around 1400, "bachelor" took on its present meaning of "unmarried man."

"Button" comes from the Old French *boton*, which is derived from a late Latin word, *buttonem*, meaning "little knob" or "stud." Buttons were originally used as decorations; they were not used to fasten clothes until about 1400, give or take a few decades. In the 1600's buttons became so ostentatious and costly that a few strict religious sects, the Amish, for example, forbade them. Even today conscientious Amish people do not use buttons. They fasten their clothes with hooks and eyes.

The name "bachelor's button" has been used for at least three different flowers. In the late 1500's and early 1600's it meant either the marsh marigold, which was bright yellow, or the deep-red double campion, also called Bleeding William.

Fashions changed, and eventually the name came to mean the deep-blue cornflower, once a wildflower that grew as a weed in Europe's cornfields. *Corn* was an old name for grain, and the flowers that grew among the grain were thus "corn flowers." Cornflowers were no source of joy to farm workers. They were troublesome weeds, sometimes choking out the grain. In bad years, so peasants believed, the devil changed grain seeds to cornflower seeds in the ground before they sprouted. Another name for the cornflower was "hurt-sickle," for the tough, woody stems of the flowers quickly dulled the soft iron of which sickles used to be made. Cornflowers must have been particularly hated at harvest time.

How the humble weed of the grain fields came to be a badge of fashion I do not know. But it was raised in gardens by the time of King Henry VIII (first half of the 1500's). Now, because of improved methods of harvesting and threshing, it is rare in the wild state and exists mostly as a garden flower.

The bachelor's button/cornflower had a long history in medicine. The Romans named it *centaurea* (also its modern scientific name) because of a legend that the centaur Chiron used it to heal a poisoned-arrow wound inflicted on him by Hercules. Since the centaurs were supposed to have taught mankind all that was known about healing herbs, the name and the legend got the bachelor's button a place in Roman apothecaries' shops.

After the downfall of the Roman Empire the cornflower went out of use, for it really has no medicinal qualities. But in the late Middle Ages it had a great revival, owing to a new medical theory called the Doctrine of Signatures. According to this mystical theory, when God created the various diseases that plague mankind, He mercifully created plants that would heal them, marking each plant with a signature to indicate the ailment it would cure. The signature was some similarity between the plant and the disease. Thus, saffron, being yellow, was supposed to be a cure for jaundice, in which the patient's skin turns yellow. The lungwort, whose leaves bear a vague resemblance to a lung, was supposed to cure lung diseases. And cornflowers, blue as the eyes of the noblest Englishman, must be God's intended remedy for eye troubles. Brown-eyed people must have had to look for a different flower.

Begonia

Begonias are native to warm, moist tropical regions. They grow wild in shady tropical forests and on rocky hillsides in South America, Central America, Asia, and Africa. They are very popular house plants, and they also make good garden flowers where the climate is damp enough. A yellow-flowered begonia that grows high in the Himalayas is used by the people of Sikkim to flavor soup.

However, there is not much to tell about the name. The begonia was named in 1706 in honor of a French colonial governor, Michel Begon (1638–1710). Begon began as a naval officer and rose to the highest rank. He later served as governor of Santa Domingo (the island that now holds Haiti and the Dominican Republic), then Louisiana, and finally Canada. He was known for his love of science and did a great deal to promote the study of botany. Perhaps he helped introduce to cultivation the flower that bears his name, but it has not been possible for me to confirm this.

31

Bluebell

Sometimes the name of a flower is beautifully descriptive. This is the case with the bluebell, whose name fits its blue, bell-shaped blossoms to perfection, no matter which of the four or five different bluebells you are speaking of. When a person in the south of England says "bluebell," he means a small, blue-flowered relative of the lily. In Scotland he would mean a species of campanula, or bellflower, also known as harebell. In the United States the chances are that he would mean the Virginia bluebell, a member of the borage family. There are also Spanish bluebells and California bluebells.

The word "blue" goes back to an old Teutonic root, *blaewo*. In the Middle Ages, when "bluebell" was first written down, it was spelled "blew." Blue, the color of the sky in good weather, is the traditional color of hope. It is also the color of fidelity, as in "true blue," and it is one of the most common colors in flags. Around 1780, "having the blue devils" was a popular slang expression in England for having a severe hangover with hallucinations. From the mood resulting from such a hangover, it also came to mean "sad" or "depressed." Both versions crossed the Atlantic and became established in America. As long ago as 1806 Noah Webster listed "dejected" as one of the meanings of "blue" in his dictionary. Washington Irving, famous for his tales of the Headless Horseman and Rip Van Winkle, seems to have been the first writer to shorten "the blue devils" to "the blues." He did this in 1807, and it has been in the language ever since. Long before the "blues" became a style of singing, it was a mood.

"Bell" comes from the Anglo-Saxon *belle*, which may come from *bellan*, the Anglo-Saxon word for "bellow." Did bells a thousand years ago in Anglo-Saxon England really bellow and roar instead of ring? It's an intriguing question. Perhaps they were so crudely made that they sounded more like an empty oil drum than a bell. Or perhaps any loud noise was a bellow to the Anglo-Saxons.

Bougainvillea

In France the man for whom the bougainvillea is named is remembered as a war hero, explorer, and scientist. Louis Antoine de Bougainville was born in Paris in 1729 and destined by his family to become a lawyer. He escaped this career by enlisting in the Regiment of Picardy, better known as the Black Musketeers. Sent to London on diplomatic duty, the young musketeer officer was elected to the Royal Society, one of the world's top-ranking scientific organizations. Bougainville earned this honor by a brilliant study of mathematics, published when he was only twenty-five.

But war broke out, and he was ordered to Canada to defend that French colony against England. When France lost the war and Canada too, Bougainville scraped together money and settlers and founded a new colony on the wind-swept Falkland Islands in the south Atlantic. Spanish pressure—the islands lie within a few days' sail of the South American mainland—forced France to abandon the colony. Bougainville, who had returned to France, was ordered to sail back to the Falkland Islands and turn the settlement over to Spain's officials. When this depressing assignment was finished, the adventurous Bougainville went on to make a round-the-world voyage, on which he explored many of the unknown islands of the Pacific. His account of the voyage and the discoveries he made became a classic.

After surrendering the Falkland Island colony to Spain, Bougainville sailed up to Rio de Janeiro to meet his supply ship. On board the supply ship was the botanist he had signed up for the expedition, a Frenchman named Commerson. While waiting for Bougainville to arrive, Commerson had kept busy by collecting tropical plants in the hills around Rio. One of them was a vine with bright, colorful blossoms, which he named Bougainvillea in honor of his chief.

The vine that bears Bougainville's name is a climber that grows many feet long. Its main stem grows into a sturdy trunk as much as a foot thick, and it is armed with wicked thorns. Its brilliant blossoms of red, purple, orange, yellow, or white make a spectacular show. (Actually they are bracts

—specialized leaves—and the true flower sits unnoticed in the center.) A member of the four o'clock family, it is native to the tropical portions of South America. To millions of people who never heard of the French soldier-explorer-scientist, it is a symbol of the tropics.

Camellia

was named for a man who probably never saw one in his life, a seventeenth-century Jesuit missionary named Georg Joseph Kamel. Kamel, whose name means "camel," was born in 1661 in the Austrian town of Brünn (now Brno, Czechoslovakia). At the time, Austria's kings also ruled Spain, so it was not strange that after Kamel became a priest he was sent to Spain's rich colony in the Far East, the Philippine Islands.

In addition to preaching to the Filipinos and their Spanish overlords Kamel set up a dispensary where poor people could get medicines free of charge. To do this, he had to become an expert on the plant life of the Philippines, for at that time the most reliable drugs were prepared from plants, and he needed good local supplies. Eventually Kamel put his botanical knowledge into a book. It may well have been the first scientific book on the plant life of the Philippines, for the Spaniards, like other colonial rulers, were interested mainly in plants that would bring them a large profit, such as sugar, rice, and tobacco.

Kamel died in 1706. Years after his death, Linnaeus decided to honor his fellow scientist by naming a plant after him. The plant he chose was a flowering shrub from Asia which bore beautiful blossoms of red, pink, or white. He gave it a Latinized version of Kamel's name, *camellia*. The choice was not entirely appropriate, for the plant came from China, while Kamel had spent his entire career in the Philippines, hundreds of miles away from the camellias' home soil. But both countries were in the Far East, and that was apparently good enough for Linnaeus.

The camellia's exact birthplace is not known, but it probably originated in China; at least, it was raised there for centuries before the Christian Era. By the eleventh century A.D. Chinese gardeners were growing seventy-two varieties of the ornamental shrub. The Japanese, who learned much of their culture from China, were also great camellia fanciers. In fact, in the seventh century a camellia mania swept Japan, and rich noblemen squandered fortunes wildly trying to outbid each other for rare and unusual varieties.

There are nearly a hundred species of camellias known to science. One of the most important is *Camellia sinensis*, the tea plant, which is raised not for its flowers but for its leaves, which are picked when young and tender, dried, and brewed in boiling water to make the well-known beverage. Tea is actually a more powerful stimulant than coffee, pound for pound, although few people would want to drink up a pound of either at one sitting.

Other species of camellias are raised for their seeds, which yield an oil that is used for cooking and hairdressing. Scientists think that camellias were originally raised for such practical products as tea and oil. Only later, when strong, prosperous societies were established, could men

38

afford to raise them just for their beauty. The camellia grows well in the southeastern United States, and it is the state flower of Alabama.

When Europeans began to trade directly with China, instead of through a chain of Middle Eastern middlemen, they tried to buy seeds of tea plants so that they could raise the valuable crop in Europe and save the huge cost of transporting the tea thousands of miles by sea or land. Dishonest Chinese merchants, not wishing to lose their monopoly, sold them seeds of ornamental camellias instead. In this way, some experts think, the first flowering camellias came to Europe. Thanks to Europeans' thirst for tea and the trickiness of a few Chinese businessmen, the camellia came to be raised in lands far beyond its native territory.

Carnation

The spicy-scented carnation has been raised for more than 2,000 years. During that time, it has picked up a good variety of names. At various times it has been known as pink, gilliflower, gillyvore, July-flower, coronation, and sops-in-wine. The name "carnation" itself is probably a shortened version of "incarnation," from the Latin *carnis*, meaning "flesh," on account of the predominant light-red color of the flowers in the old days. Another theory is that "carnation" is a corruption of "coronation," because lovers in ancient Rome sometimes wore wreaths of carnation blossoms on their heads. (The Latin word *corona* means "wreath" as well as "crown.")

The word "carnation" first appeared in English in the early 1530's as the name of a shade of light red or flesh color. A few years later it turned up as the name of the flower that now bears it; so the most likely guess is that the flower was named for the color.

The name "pink" dates from the late 1500's. It refers, not to the color of the flower, but to the scalloped, jagged edges of the petals, and it comes from an old word meaning to prick or to stab. Today we still talk of "pinking" the edge of a piece of cloth, and it is usually done with special "pinking shears."

The color pink is named after the flower. (However, the expression "the pink of perfection" does not come from the carnation. It is a corruption of a much older form, "the pervynke of perfection." *Pervynke* was an old name for the periwinkle.)

In his plays Shakespeare spoke of both pinks and carnations. He also used the much older name "gilliflower," which can be traced back to the 1300's. "Gillyflower" comes from the Old French name for cloves, *girofle* or *gilofre*, which comes from the Latin name *caryophyllum*. This is a Latinized version of the Greek name for cloves, *karyophyllon*, which rather illogically comes from *karyon* ("nut") plus *phyllon* ("leaf"). Actually cloves are not nuts at all, but the dried flower buds of a tropical tree belonging to the myrtle family. Although carnations and cloves are not related, many types of carnation have a strong clove fragrance, and from Roman times until fairly recently they were used as substitutes for cloves.

Carnations probably originated in the Mediterranean region and spread from there until wild species of carnation

41

were growing in Eurasia as far north as Siberia and as far east as Japan. A few species are also native to Africa and the far north of North America. Exactly how long they have been cultivated is not known, but the ancient Greeks grew them and called them *dianthos*, meaning "God's flower," for they believed them to be sacred to Zeus. The modern scientific name of the genus to which carnations belong is *Dianthus*, a Latinized version of the old Greek name.

The Roman historian Pliny wrote—mistakenly—that the spicy-scented carnation known as the clove pink was discovered in Spain during the reign of the Emperor Augustus (27 B.C.–A.D. 14). But he was right when he reported that the flowers were used to flavor wine and other beverages. Englishmen in Queen Elizabeth's time used clove pinks the same way, from which came the nickname "sops-in-wine."

During the 1600's carnations were used in medicines and made into a kind of jam that was said to be good for the heart. They were also used in desserts, made into relish, and candied by dipping them into egg white and powdered sugar. Nowadays carnations are used in perfume. Because they last well when cut, they are popular for bouquets. They are also one of the most popular garden flowers, and more than 2,000 varieties are raised.

Ohio has the scarlet carnation for its state flower. The most common colors of carnations are pink, red, and white, but there are also yellow and purple varieties, as well as striped ones. The green carnations sold on St. Patrick's Day are dyed, however.

Carnations were raised mainly as a flavoring until the late 1500's, when they suddenly zoomed into popularity as ornamental flowers. By the early 1600's they were the most popular garden flower in England. By the 1700's several hundred distinct varieties were being grown in England alone, with such colorful names as Beazarts, Painted Ladies, Bleeding Swain, and Fiery Trial. Flower fanciers held carnation competitions. So that the flowers would appear at their best, they were permitted to remove all deformed, badly marked, and superfluous petals, after which the remaining petals were arranged as carefully as a beautiful woman's hairdo. Wealthy people could hire specialists to fix their flowers for them, and a certain barber named Kit Nunn was kept as busy dressing flowers as he was dressing wigs.

Once upon a time, well-dressed men liked to start the day with a fresh carnation in the lapels of their jackets, fastened through a special buttonhole made just for that purpose. A flower worn like this was called a *boutonniere* (French for "buttonhole"). Fashions changed, and although the buttonholes are still found in the lapels of the better grades of jackets, the flowers are no longer seen.

One of the last stands of the boutonniere was in the lapel of the department-store floorwalker, a store official who acted as a roving troubleshooter. Wearing a carnation (usually white) as his badge of office, he would patrol his section of the floor, seeing that everything was running smoothly. If a customer was having trouble with a surly or incompetent clerk, or if a nasty customer was taking out her aggressions on a helpless salesperson (in those days a man was seldom seen shopping in a department store), the floor-walker would discreetly hasten to the scene and smooth the trouble out. The floorwalker also answered questions from shoppers and did his best to make shopping pleasant. About the time of the Korean War (1950) floorwalkers began to disappear, and now they are about as plentiful as the blue whale and the whooping crane.

Strangely—or perhaps not so strangely—the floorwalker may be connected with the decline of the boutonniere. When a young man tried to spruce up with a carnation in his buttonhole, his friends seldom missed the chance to tease him unmercifully, asking him if he'd just gotten a job as a floorwalker. This was enough to kill almost anyone's enthusiasm for buttonhole flowers, and, as the younger generation grew up and became the older generation, the boutonniere gradually vanished. But—who can tell—another swing in fashion may bring it back again.

Chrysanthemum

literally means "golden flower." Its name comes from the Greek *chrysanthemon,* from *chrysos,* "gold," plus *anthos,* "flower." It is the name of a genus of flowers that includes about 150 species, including the common daisy. All the chrysanthemums belong to the giant plant family called *Compositae.* Their relatives include the sunflower, black-eyed Susan, zinnia, dahlia, marigold, aster, thistle, artichoke, and lettuce.

Chrysanthemums are native to Europe, Asia, and North America. The flower known today as the chrysanthemum is a cross between two Chinese species. It has been cultivated for more than 2,000 years, and Confucius is thought to have referred to it in his writings about 2,500 years ago.

In England the name "chrysanthemum" was first used in the late 1500's for a European species also known as the Corn Marigold. The bright yellow flowers of this plant made it a natural choice for some Elizabethan botanist's poetic flight of fancy. In the late 1700's Englishmen were importing flowers from the Far East for their gardens, and the name was shifted to the Oriental species that we now call chrysanthemum.

Unlike many flowers in ancient times, most of the chrysanthemums were grown purely for decoration. One European species, the fever-few, was used in medicine. Its name is an Anglo-Saxon corruption of the Latin name *febrifugia*, meaning "fever chaser." Not only was the flower used in treating fevers, but in the 1600's it was used to counteract the effects of an overdose of opium. Doctors of the period also recommended it for dizziness and melancholia. In Italy it was eaten in salads and also fried with eggs.

Probably the world's greatest chrysanthemum growers are the Japanese, who first got the flower from China around the end of the fourth century A.D. About 300 years later, it was made the personal emblem of the Japanese emperors, and for many centuries only the emperors and the nobility were allowed to have it in their gardens. The chrysanthemum is still the imperial emblem and the national flower of Japan.

The Oriental chrysanthemum did not reach Europe until the late 1600's, and European gardeners did not learn how to grow it successfully for another century. But in the 1800's plant breeders developed spectacular new varieties, aided by botanist-explorers who brought back new strains from China and Japan. The huge pompon chrysanthemums sold at football games were developed in this way. They are descended from the small poms developed in France around 1850 and named for the pompons (small tufts) that French soldiers wore on their hats.

Chrysanthemums come in such a variety of colors, sizes, and shapes that it is impossible to describe them all. Some bloom in the summer, while other varieties bloom in the fall and keep on producing flowers until a heavy frost kills them off. Chrysanthemums are popular for bouquets because they last very well, and florists have learned how to make them flower at any season by controlling the amount of light they get. Thus, they are available the year around.

Chrysanthemums do not come true from seed—that is, the flowers that come from the seeds do not look like their parent flowers. Because of this, they must be propagated by dividing (that is, by splitting up a clump of roots and stems into several new plants) or from cuttings. In this method the tops, plus a short section of the stem, are snipped off and stuck into moist sand until they grow roots. Then they can be transplanted to pot or garden.

Raising chrysanthemums is a big business. Millions of dollars' worth of chrysanthemum plants and cut flowers are sold every year, keeping growers, florists, and plant breeders happy. Yellow, white, pink, lavender, bronze, or any other color, to the flower industry it is truly the "golden flower."

Clematis

What does the high-climbing, spectacular clematis, with its huge flowers of a dozen shades, have in common with the humble buttercup? You're right. They are related. Both are members of the buttercup family, known to botanists as the *Ranunculaceae*. This family name comes from the Latin name for the buttercup, *ranunculus*, meaning "little frog." I do not know why this name was chosen—perhaps because buttercups grow best in wet, marshy soil, where frogs also thrive. Some other members of the family are peonies, delphiniums, anemones, and Christmas roses.

There are nearly 200 known species of clematis found in nature, and there are gardeners' varieties too numerous to count. Clematises are native to Europe, Asia, northern Africa, and North America. They grow from ten to thirty feet tall, depending on variety. A clematis vine climbs by means of its leaves, which hook down over any handy projection and give their stalks a twist to hold tight. This is an unusual trick, for climbing plants usually climb by rootlets that hold tight (for example, ivy); tendrils (grapevines); or by winding around a tree trunk or other support (morning glory and wisteria). Clematis flowers, which in some varieties measure up to eight inches across, may be blue, white, purple, pink, red, yellow, and any number of shades in between.

The name "Clematis," from the Greek *klema*, meaning "vine branch," was bestowed on the flower in the late 1500's. As so often happens, rival botanists decided to apply the name to a different flower, the periwinkle, a trailing plant with small blue or white flowers, which made things pretty confusing. However, the name "clematis" is no longer used for the periwinkle.

Homeowners like to use clematis for covering rain pipes, fences, mailbox posts, sides of buildings, and bare patches of ground. Clematis will grow almost anywhere, but it needs plenty of sun to flower.

After the flowers have bloomed out and dropped off, feathery, silvery-colored seed heads remain on the vine, waiting for a strong wind to pick up the winged seeds and carry them off. Their appearance has given rise to such folk names as "old man's beard" and "virgin's bower" (possibly referring to the Virgin Mary, to whom so many flowers were dedicated). In Britain another name for the clematis was "traveler's joy," for its gay blossoms by the wayside must have cheered weary travelers in the days when a trip was more torture than pleasure.

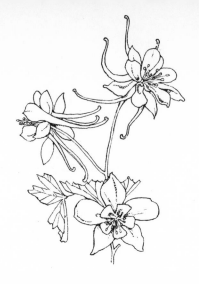

Columbine

"Columbine" comes from the Latin *columbinus,* meaning "dovelike," which is derived from *columba,* the Latin word for "dove." It entered the English language in the Middle Ages by way of the French *colombine,* although columbines had been growing wild in England for uncounted centuries before then. The name is derived from the resemblance of the blossoms—when viewed from a certain angle—to a dove with outspread wings.

The dove is a symbol of peace, yet the scientific name of the flower, *aquilegia,* comes from *aquila,* the Latin name for the eagle, emblem of many a fierce and warlike conqueror. Eagle and dove, war and peace, both symbolized by the same flower, which happens to look a little bit like a bird with its wings spread! People can interpret the same thing in very different ways.

The columbine belongs to the buttercup family, along with the clematis, peony, Christmas rose, and, of course, the buttercup itself. Columbines grow wild over most of the northern hemisphere, and there are many species. One—the Rocky Mountain columbine—is the state flower of Colorado.

Columbines were very popular during the Middle Ages. The great English poet Chaucer, who lived in the 1300's, loved columbines so much that he used them as symbols in his poetry. At least one nobleman was so fond of the flower that he put it in his coat of arms. During the Middle Ages, columbines were used in medicine—they were an ingredient in a remedy for the plague in 1373—and in cooking, where they were used to color jelly. Down to the mid-1700's columbine seeds were used in remedies for measles, smallpox, and jaundice. About that time people began to fear that the seeds were poisonous (in fact, the buttercup family has many poisonous members) and prudently stopped using them.

Crocus

The crocus, one of the earliest flowers to bloom in the spring, was first raised as a spice plant. The spice was saffron, the pungent orange-yellow flavoring, which is actually the dried stigmas of one species of crocus. The very name of the crocus comes from the ancient Greek name for saffron, which was *krokos*. The Greeks in turn probably borrowed the name from one of the Semitic languages related to Hebrew and Arabic. In Hebrew, *karkom* means both "saffron" and "crocus," and one of the Arabic words for saffron is *kurkum*; another is *zafaran*, from which our word "saffron" comes.

Greeks, Jews, and Arabs all traded busily with each other in the eastern Mediterranean lands, and they picked up many words from each other. Where the name originally came from no one knows, for the saffron crocus has been cultivated for so long that all traces of its origin have been lost. Botanists believe that the crocus originated somewhere in the Near East, but that is about all they can tell us.

More than 4,000 years ago, the island of Crete was a center of saffron production, and saffron was sacred to the great goddess of Crete, Britomartis. More than 3,000 years ago the Egyptians were using saffron as a drug to treat rheumatism and dental trouble.

The Greeks used saffron chiefly as a dye. Because of its high cost, it was used to color the robes of kings. To the Greeks saffron was so precious that their poets described the robes of the Greek gods as saffron-colored. They had good reason for this, for saffron is one of the costliest of all spices to produce. About 4,300 crocus blossoms must be gathered, and their stamens carefully removed and dried, to make one single ounce of the deep yellow-orange spice. And each step must be done by hand.

Like the Greeks, the ancient Irish considered saffron a royal color. The Hindus used it in religious ceremonies, and today saffron is one of the colors in the flag of India.

The Romans used saffron as a dye and a perfume. At the notorious banquets that wealthy Romans gave to display their riches, pastries were sometimes drenched with costly saffron sauce to impress the guests. Sometimes saffron was sprinkled on the floor between courses to freshen the air with its scent. Even the richest Romans could not afford to use pure saffron so lavishly, however, so the saffron was mixed with vermilion to give it a brighter color, mica flakes to make it glitter, and large amounts of sawdust to make it go farther. It was probably the Romans who introduced the saffron crocus to western Europe and Britain, to increase the supply by opening up new areas to cultivation. The saffron crocus seems to have disappeared during the Dark Ages after the Roman Empire broke down, but it was brought back from the Near East by crusaders during the 1200's or 1300's.

Saffron again became an important crop in certain localities where the flowers grew well. During the Middle Ages, adulterating saffron (mixing it with other substances to cheat the customer) was regarded as a particularly vicious crime. In Germany dishonest spice dealers were sometimes burned alive in the marketplace together with their adulterated saffron, and once three men were buried alive for the same offense. It was probably not just the high price of saffron that made the punishment so severe, but ancient traditions of the plant's sacredness.

Up into the 1700's saffron crocuses were raised on a large scale in England. They even gave their name to a town, Saffron Walden, which has three crocus flowers in its coat of arms. The workers who cultivated the crocus fields were called "crokers," and some took Croker as a family name.

The most famous person to bear that name was Richard Croker, a notorious boss of New York City's corrupt political machine, Tammany Hall. As Tammany's leader, Croker was able to loot the city treasury of a large fortune. In 1901, with prosecution threatening him, he hastily retired from politics and vanished, emerging in Ireland as the owner of a magnificent estate and a fine stable of racing horses.

Although the saffron crocus and a few other species bloom in the fall, most of our garden crocuses bloom in the spring. They are a traditional sign of spring's arrival, like the first appearance of the swallows and the ice-cream man.

It was once believed that saffron "provoked laughter and merriment." An overdose was believed to cause death by laughing. Saffron was used down to the 1600's for hangovers, jaundice, and measles. A bag of saffron worn over the pit of the stomach was thought to prevent seasickness. Since seasickness is caused as much by psychological factors as by anything else, this may have worked—sometimes.

The flower known as the "autumn crocus" is actually not related to the crocuses. It belongs to the lily family, whereas crocuses belong to the iris family. Its botanical name is *Colchicum*, from the ancient city of Colchis, where the legendary Argonauts went to seek the Golden Fleece. The plant yields a powerful drug, colchicine, which is used in treating gout, a painful disease of the toe and other joints.

Seventeenth-century chemists gave the name "crocus powder" to various reddish-yellow substances they obtained by heating metals. (The color of the chemical resembled saffron.) The crocus powders were used for a time in medicine; one form is now used for putting a fine polish on metal.

In the late 1700's, English army and navy surgeons were nicknamed "crocus," probably from the crocus powders they dealt out to their luckless patients. Eventually the name degenerated to "croaker," an apt comment on these men's medical skills, for by then "croak" had become a synonym for "die." But it is only fair to remember that the name comes from the chemical laboratory, not from the crocus flower.

Daffodil

is the name given to a kind of narcissus. (Some people use the name for all narcissi—see the entry for Narcissus for the details.) Although the daffodil grows wild over most of Europe, it had no name at all in English until the 1500's, when people began to call it "affodyl," a corruption of the *asphodel* of classic Greek mythology. The asphodel is a kind of lily with grayish leaves and pallid yellow flowers that grows wild in the Mediterranean region. No one is sure what the name originally meant, but some people have guessed that it came from *spodos*, the Greek word for "ashes," because of the plant's coloring. In very early times among the Greeks the poor people ate asphodel roots, which they foraged from wild plants growing in woods and meadows, while the rich feasted on barley porridge. In later Greek my-

59

thology asphodels became the food of the dead, while the barley porridge, called *ambrosia*, was changed beyond recognition into the indescribably delicious food of the gods.

Perhaps because of its ghostly appearance, the asphodel very early became the chief flower of the dead. Homer, who lived about 3,000 years ago, described asphodel-covered meadows where the souls of the dead wandered, and this became a stock image of Greek poets. Asphodels were planted on graves, and the goddess Persephone—who spent half the year in the underworld, thus causing winter on the earth—wore a gloomy floral crown of asphodels on her head. On a more worldly level the Greeks used asphodel as a cure for snakebites and a charm against sorcery. They also believed that it poisoned mice and protected pigs against disease.

Around 1530 a white variety of asphodel was imported into England to grace the gardens of the nobility. After a few years people were also using the name "asphodel" for white narcissus, and a generation later "affodyl" meant any narcissus. The "d" was probably added to the beginning of the word to make a playful nickname, and the nickname soon replaced the original word. From "daffodil" came another version, "daffadowndilly," which remained a country name for the flower until recent times.

Elizabethan writers fell in love with the daffodil, which their forefathers had ignored. They put it into gardens and garden manuals, poetry and plays. Shakespeare himself used daffodils in several famous lines. One of the most delightful of these comes from a song in *The Winter's Tale*:

> When daffodils begin to peer,
> With heigh! the doxy o'er the dale
> Why, then comes in the sweet of the year
> For the red blood reigns in the winter's pale.

Even the fact that these lines are sung by a thieving confidence man cannot spoil their charm.

Dahlia

In 1519 the Spanish conquistador Hernan Cortes marched triumphantly into Mexico City at the head of his armored cavalrymen and musketeers. If the Spaniards had not been so busy looking for gold and jewels, they might have noticed a red, daisylike flower growing in the beautiful gardens of the Aztecs. This was the ancestor of our modern dahlia.

The Aztecs, who were the greatest gardeners of all the American Indian peoples, called the dahlia *cocoxochitl*. (*Xochitl* is the Aztec word for "flower.") In addition to growing it for decoration, they used it in medicines. But the Spaniards ignored the dahlia, although they spread some of the Aztecs' plants, such as the tomato, the pineapple, and the avocado to other parts of their empire. The dahlia was not a food plant; it yielded no fiber that could be spun into cloth or twisted into rope; no spices could be made from it. It was not even a particularly spectacular flower. In fact, it was rather dull.

Not until 1789 did the dahlia reach Europe, when a Spanish botanist in Mexico City sent seeds to a friend in Spain. The friend, a priest-botanist, set to work improving the flower, and he soon had some showy blossoms on hand. Pleased with his success, he christened the flower in honor of a Swedish botanist named Andreas Dahl, who is known to history only as a pupil of the great Linnaeus.

The exotic new flower from far-off Mexico soon found highborn admirers in Europe. The aristocratic wife of the English ambassador to Spain sent the first dahlias to England. In France the Empress Josephine, imperial consort of Napoleon, grew dahlias in her palace garden. It is whispered that she actually planted some with her own hands, which in those days was considered quite far out for a person of high rank.

New varieties were developed with dizzying speed: scarlet, pink, crimson, lavender, dark purple, orange, yellow, salmon pink, and a rainbow of other shades, with blossoms ranging from two inches across to the size of a dinner plate. Today there are over 3,000 varieties.

The dahlia belongs to the *Compositae* family, which includes the chrysanthemum and many other well-known garden flowers. The common garden dahlias grow from four to six feet tall (there are also dwarf types that grow only knee-high), but in the dahlia's homeland of Mexico and Central America there are species that grow to the size of trees, twenty feet tall and more.

It is said that the Indians of Mexico ate the fleshy roots of the dahlia before they learned to cultivate corn. On the strength of this tradition, some European scientists in the eighteenth century hoped that the dahlia could be developed into a useful vegetable like the potato. However, neither human beings nor livestock would touch the bitter roots. Although edible, they were not palatable, no matter how they were doctored.

Later on it was learned that dahlia roots are a good source of levulose, a form of sugar used in medicine for people who cannot digest ordinary sugar. Before the discovery of insulin in the 1920's, doctors used to prescribe levulose for patients suffering from diabetes, and some of this was made from dahlias. The petals of dahlias can also be eaten in salads. Health-food enthusiasts please take note!

Daisy

comes from the Anglo-Saxon *daeges eage*, or "day's eye," referring to the flower's habit of opening in the morning and closing at night. But the flower that the Anglo-Saxons named so poetically was not our American daisy, which stays open round the clock, but its relative, the English daisy, a small flower growing only three to six inches tall, with crimson tips on its white petals. This flower grows wild in fields and lawns in Britain, where it is as much of a pest as dandelions are in the United States. (Both the American daisy and the English daisy belong to the family of *Compositae*.)

The American daisy is actually a chrysanthemum. Its scientific name is *Chrysanthemum leucanthemum*, or "white-flowered chrysanthemum," from the Greek *leukos*, "white," and *anthos*, "flower." Other names for it are "ox-eye daisy" and "whiteweed." Native to Europe and Asia, it probably came to America with early European colonists, its seeds hitching a ride in hay used for packing their belongings in rough wooden chests. When the white man cleared away the forest to make fields and pastureland, the daisy found a ready-made home. In fact, it succeeded so well that it came to be regarded as a weed. Farmers hated it because it made their cows give bitter, bad-tasting milk.

With its ring of petals surrounding a bright yellow disk, the daisy must have suggested the sun to many ancient peoples and so took on a supernatural significance. Four thousand years ago, the artists of the great Minoan civilization, which flourished on the island of Crete, used daisies in the designs of the ornaments they turned out. The Assyrians, whose empire dominated the Near East for nearly 300 years, used daisies in a formula for turning gray hair black. They also brewed a medicine for eye troubles from the daisy.

In Wales during the Middle Ages daisies were used to remove warts, to cure insanity, and to treat smallpox, tumors, jaundice, boils, and skin diseases. In England itself (then quite separate from Wales) people brewed remedies from daisies to treat bruises and broken bones. From this came the old folk names "bruisewort" and "banewort." ("Wort" was an old name for plants used for food or medicine. "Bane" was a northern English form of "bone.") The English daisy was also used to stop the flow of blood from wounds, hence its scientific name of *Bellis*, from the Latin *bellum*, meaning "war." At times daisies were even eaten: fifteenth-century recipes list them among the ingredients for a salad.

Noblemen often used daisies in their coats of arms, and a queen of England, Margaret of Anjou (1430–82) had three ox-eye daisies in her own coat of arms. Born and raised in

France, she called herself Marguerite rather than Margaret, and *marguerite* is the French name for the ox-eye daisy to this day. Was the daisy named after the queen, or did she pick it for her coat of arms because it already shared her name? It's an interesting case for word hunters to crack. Incidentally, Marguerite and all other forms of Margaret are derived from the Greek word for pearl, *margaron*.

The Germans are not as romantic about the daisy as the French. They call it *Gänseblume*, or "goose-flower." But they call the English daisy *Tausendschön*, or "thousand times beautiful," which almost makes up for it. In Sweden the daisy is called *prästkrage*, or "priest's collar," because it looks like the big ruffled collars that Swedish Lutheran ministers used to wear.

In the language of flowers daisies stood for innocence. In the slang of the 1890's, "daisy" came to mean something first-rate, as in: "See my new bike! Isn't it a daisy?" On the grimmer side, "pushing up the daisies" and a clutch of similar expressions meant "dead."

Like Rose, Lily, Iris, and Violet, Daisy is one of the flower names given to girls. According to the dictionary, it is sometimes a nickname for Candace or Margaret (shades of Queen Margaret of Anjou and her ox-eye daisies!). Now rather uncommon, it was once extremely popular. Back in the 1890's, a young songwriter named Harry Dacre, composing a song about a bicycle built for two, picked Daisy for the name of the song's heroine. The song was an immediate hit, and Daisy is still musically looking sweet upon the seat of her tandem bike, though by now she must be a great-grandmother.

Everyone knows the old game of she-loves-me-she-loves-me-not, in which one measures a sweetheart's affection by pulling petals off a daisy. This game goes back to a time when people saw signs of their fate in all kinds of everyday things. As an emblem of fidelity the daisy was a natural choice for telling one's fortune in love. But there may be a more practical reason: The daisy usually has an odd number of petals; so if you are clever enough to begin with "loves me," the answer is almost certain to come out right.

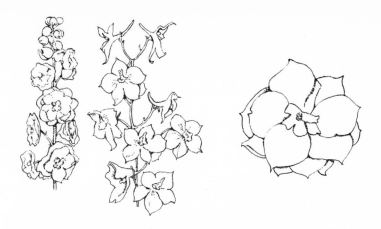

Delphinium

The delphinium is found in nature over all the northern temperate regions of the world, but its name comes from Greece. The ancient Greeks thought that its flowers looked like leaping dolphins, which they knew from their voyages around the Mediterranean Sea, and they named them *delphinion,* or "little dolphin," from *delphin,* "dolphin." The dolphin, sacred to the god Apollo, was important in Greek mythology. The Greeks also believed that dolphins would rescue drowning sailors and carry them to shore.

Later European peoples had their own names for the Greeks' dolphin flower, often derived from the spurlike projection at the rear of the blossom. (The Greeks would have said the spur was the dolphin's snout). The Germans, for example, called it *Rittersporn;* the Spaniards, *espuela de caballero;* and the Swedes, *riddarsporre*—all meaning "knight's spur." The English called it "larkspur" because it reminded them of the long hind claw on a lark's foot. Seventeenth-century botanists, trained in the classics, picked up the old Greek name, tacked on the Latin ending -*um*, and the deed was done: Delphinium became the official name. The old folk names are still thriving, however.

The delphinium belongs to the buttercup family, and there are about 250 species. Blue is the most usual color, but there are also pink, white, purple, red, and yellow delphiniums.

One species of delphinium, no longer cultivated, was called "stavesacre," an English corruption of the Latin *staphisagria*, which the Romans appropriated from the Greek *staphis agria*, meaning "wild raisins." The poisonous seeds of the stavesacre were ground up and dusted on children's hair to kill lice and fleas. They were also used as an emetic (a drug that makes the patient vomit) and to cure toothaches.

The larkspur was for a long time used to treat wounds, and the juice of the flowers was believed to strengthen the eyesight. In the 1600's, some Europeans even believed that simply looking at the flowers was enough to help their failing eyes, and they hung big bunches of them in their rooms for this purpose. Another superstition was that the "larks heele" was an antidote to poison, and that if it were placed in front of a scorpion or other venomous creature, the animal would be paralyzed and unable to do harm until the flower was taken away. It is not recorded if anyone put this belief to the test of actual use. If he did, he was painfully disappointed.

Forget-me-not

owes its name to an old European belief that those who wore the flowers would not be forgotten by their lovers. The belief probably originated in France, for the oldest of the names for the flower is French, *ne m'oubliez mye* ("don't forget me" in Old French). The English "forget-me-not" is a translation of the French name. So are the names of the forget-me-not in many other European languages, such as the German *Vergiss-mein-nicht*, the Spanish *nomeolvides*, and the Swedish *förgät-mig-ej*.

Once this superstition was firmly established in folk beliefs, numerous legends came into being to "explain" it. One of the most fatuous was the tale of a German knight who was out riding with his lady love when her kerchief blew into a river. The maiden shed scalding tears of sorrow at the loss of her precious silken kerchief, dyed with the costliest dyes of the East. At her request, the knight, clad though he was in full armor, gallantly plunged into the river to recover the silken bauble. Of course, the weight of the armor dragged him under, and he drowned. With his last breath of life he cried out, "Forget me not!" On the river's marshy bank, a plant with hundreds of tiny, blue flowers sprang up to preserve his memory, for blue is the color of remembrance. The repentant maiden spent the rest of her life watering them with her tears.

Poetic as some of these legends may be, the name "forget-me-not" was used for three or four plants that looked rather alike: low, spreading, and covered with tiny blue flowers. Around 1800, botanists and poets ended the confusion by agreeing that the *real* forget-me-not was the flower which the Greeks called *myosotis*, or "mouse-ear," from the size and shape of its leaves. This is now its scientific name.

The romantic revival of the 1800's made the forget-me-not popular. Parisian florists sold them by the bunch and by the potful for gifts of "love and remembrance." The Germans often planted them around graves. By the 1870's the forget-me-not was also a popular garden flower. It is also the state flower of Alaska.

An old name for the forget-me-not was "scorpion grass" or "scorpion flower," since some people saw a resemblance between the flower heads and a scorpion's tail. By the doctrine

of sympathetic magic, it followed that the juice of the plant must cure scorpion stings. (It does not.) In some regions, forget-me-nots were used in vain attempts to cure the bites of snakes and mad dogs. They were also mashed up and used as a poultice for inflamed eyes and boiled in milk and water to make a remedy for dysentery. One superstition had it that a steel blade tempered in the juice of the forget-me-not was so hard it could cut through stone without being dulled.

Most species of forget-me-not have hairy stalks. Botanists believed that the plant developed these hairs to keep ants from crawling up the stems to eat the nectar, for these flowers need their nectar to attract the flying insects that pollinate them.

The forget-me-not's bright blue flowers with a contrasting

yellow circle in the middle fascinated an eighteenth-century German botanist named Sprengel. He wondered if there might not be some purpose to this arrangement. After a good deal of study he came to the conclusion that the color scheme of the flower served as a signal to guide insects to the heart of the flower, where pollination was accomplished. From this starting point he went on to work out the first theory of the ways in which flowers and insects had evolved in cooperation with each other. Thus, the modest flower with the romantic legend rendered a real service to science.

Forsythia

is a native of China, Japan, and Korea. One of the first shrubs to bloom in the spring, the forsythia adds a welcome touch of color to drab northern parks and gardens. Its sunny yellow blossoms have given it the nickname "golden bells."

The forsythia is a member of the olive family, and its relatives include the lilac, the privet (a bush used for hedges), the jasmine, known for its sweet scent, and the ash tree, known for making the finest baseball bats.

The forsythia has almost unbelievable vitality. Given half a chance, a forsythia bush will spread with amazing speed.

Not only does it send up forests of new stems from the roots, but the branches, bending over to touch the ground, take root at their tips and send up new sprouts in turn. In a few years, a skimpy little forsythia bush can turn into a miniature jungle. Children love to play cave under the arching branches of a big old forsythia bush. Dogs and cats like to lie there, too, out of the heat of the summer sun.

The forsythia was named for the man who introduced it to England, William Forsyth. Born in Scotland in 1737, Forsyth began his career as a gardener's assistant, but worked his way up until, in middle life, he became director of the famous Chelsea Physic Garden at London. This garden belonged to the Apothecaries' Company of London, and great quantities of medicinal herbs were raised there. It was a position of great responsibility and prestige. In 1784 Forsyth rose as far as a gardener could hope to rise in eighteenth-century England. He became superintendent of the Royal Gardens at the palaces of St. James and Kensington. The forsythia was named after him in 1788.

In his own time, Forsyth was better known as the author of a famous book on the care of trees and the inventor of a patent remedy for tree wounds, which he called a "plaister." It was composed of lime, manure, ashes, soapsuds, urine, and various other ingredients, and Forsyth claimed that it would heal tree wounds, banish rot, and restore sick and dying trees, even those so rotted out that only the bark remained. The British government, desperate to increase its supply of timber for warships, purchased a large order of the compound, and gullible members of Parliament gratefully voted him a reward and a medal. However, the "plaister" somehow failed to do the things Forsyth claimed it would do, and a nasty scandal blew up. Forsyth died in 1804, in the middle of it. The scandal is now forgotten, while we still have the bright, golden flowers of the forsythia to remind us of the Scottish gardener who made good.

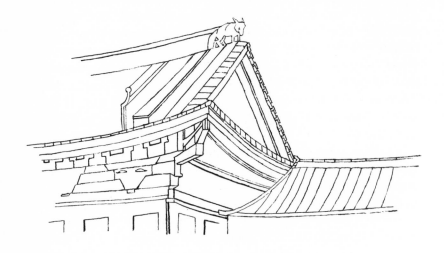

Foxglove

is a flower whose name is linked with the lore of magic and mystery. The name comes from the Anglo-Saxon *foxes glofa*, or "foxes' gloves." The connection with foxes is not clear, but the fox has a long tradition of magical powers in many lands. In China and Japan foxes are credited with the power to transform themselves into human beings. In Japan, as late as World War II, department stores and other public buildings had fox shrines on their roofs, where women could propitiate the malicious fox spirits that might otherwise harm them.

"Fox," according to scholars, comes from an ancient Indo-European root meaning "the bushy-tailed one." An old legend tells how men once slaughtered foxes for their tails, which were a potent charm against the devil. The desperate foxes begged God for protection, and he put bell-shaped flowers in the fields to ring whenever hunters approached. Thus warned, the foxes were able to scurry off to safe hiding places. When the danger was ended, the flower bells lost their sound.

Another legend says that the fairies gave the flowers to the foxes to wear on their feet when they raided chicken-coops at night. With magical powers, they enabled the foxes to creep up on their prey silently.

The foxglove is closely connected to fairies in old folk beliefs. In fact, one theory is that the name is really "folk's glove," since the blossoms were worn as mittens by the "wee folk"—the fairies. In Ireland they were called "fairy thimbles" and in Wales "goblin's gloves." The Scots called them "dead men's bells" and whispered that if you heard them ring you had not long to live. In England, as late as Shakespeare's time, country people thought that a foxglove blossom was likely to conceal a sleeping fairy. This was no joke to the superstitious countryman, for to him fairies were not just a quaint fancy. He was convinced that they were real, and he was just as convinced that they had no love for mankind. At the slightest provocation they would take a malicious revenge, sometimes even killing the offender.

Some students of mythology think that there really were fairies, but they were not supernatural beings small enough to hide in a flower. Instead, they were human beings of a small, dark race that inhabited the British Isles before Celts, Romans, Anglo-Saxons, and Normans overran their country. Defeated by the larger, stronger, and better-armed strangers, the "little folk" retreated to wild mountain and forest strongholds, where they lived in underground shelters to escape detection and stole out at night to raid the fields and homes of the invaders. As the "little folk" gradually died out, stories about them were mingled with the usual peasant tales of spooks and goblins until they became mythical creatures themselves.

Not all the names for the foxglove reflected its sinister association with fairies. One of the French names for the flower is *doigt de la Vierge*, or "Virgin Mary's finger." The Swedish name is *fingerborgsblomma*, or "thimbleflower," and the German name is *Fingerhut*, or just plain "thimble." We owe the scientific name of the flower to a sixteenth-century German botanist, who simply translated the German *Fingerhut* into the medieval Latin word for "thimble," *Digitalis*. The ultimate root of *digitalis* is the Latin *digitus*, "finger." By coincidence, the botanist's name was Fuchs—the German word for "fox."

The ancient Greeks and Romans used the juice of the foxglove for sprains and bruises. In medieval times foxglove was one of the flowers that witches raised in their gardens for brewing magical potions. Causing death by undetectable means was one of the witches' most lucrative specialties, and foxglove yields a chemical, digitalin, which in large doses causes heart failure. In legitimate medieval medicine, foxgloves were used to treat a skin disease called scrofula, from which comes the scientific name of the family to which they belong, *Scrophularaceae*.

In the late 1700's an English physician discovered that a tea brewed from foxglove leaves helped patients suffering from dropsy, a disease in which water accumulates in the body tissues and makes the victim swell up like a balloon. Dropsy is not only unsightly; it is crippling, for the victim's legs may swell so badly that he cannot move. But the foxglove tea acted to stimulate the patient's kidneys so that he could get rid of the excess water in his body. Later an even more important use was discovered when doctors noticed that dropsy patients drinking foxglove tea had their heartbeats slowed and strengthened. Today digitalin, prepared from the foxglove, is still a major drug for treating heart trouble. Perhaps there is a little bit of magic in the foxglove after all.

Gardenia

The name "gardenia" commemorates a fashionable eighteenth-century Charleston doctor, Alexander Garden. Born in Aberdeenshire, Scotland in 1730, Garden came to South Carolina as a young man of twenty-three. He settled in the thriving port of Charleston, at that time one of the leading cities in Britain's American colonies. Wealthy merchants shipped rice, tobacco, and indigo to Britain. The great planters from whose estates these products came maintained sumptuous town houses in Charleston for the social season. Garden, a handsome and charming young man, fitted easily into the cultured, leisurely world of Charleston, and despite his youth soon became a popular society doctor. He must also have been a skillful physician, for looks and charm can't carry a doctor very far if his patients don't get better.

Garden's need for medicinal plants got him involved in the study of botany, and from there he became passionately interested in every phase of natural history. He exchanged news for many years with the great Swedish botanist Linnaeus, and he also collected American plants and animals for his many scientist friends in Europe. It was he who sent the first specimens of the electric eel to Europe. Garden also discovered the Congo eel and the mud eel.

His pleasant existence was ended by the outbreak of the American Revolution. A loyal Tory, Garden sided with the British; and when his side lost, he left the country, never to return. His son fought on the American side, and Garden never forgave him.

Garden lived out the rest of his life in England, mostly as an invalid. Before he died in 1791, he served briefly as a vice president of the Royal Society, one of the oldest and most important scientific societies in the world.

Garden may never have seen the flower named in his honor. It was brought to Europe, and later to the United States, from China and Japan. A member of the madder family, it has some interesting relatives. One is the coffee tree; another is ipecacuanha, a South American plant that yields the drug ipecac, used in medicine to make patients vomit. Another member of the family is madder, formerly one of the leading sources of red and brown dyes for cloth. Most of the plants of the family are tropical, and the gardenia itself cannot stand frost. In regions with cold winters, gardenias must be grown in pots so that they can be brought indoors when cold weather comes, or else in greenhouses.

The gardenia plant is an evergreen bush that under favorable conditions grows six feet tall. In parts of the South it is planted outdoors to make hedges. The leaves are dark green and glossy. The flowers are white and have a delightful sweet scent. Although they do not last long, the flowers are used in corsages and bridal bouquets. They are also used in perfume.

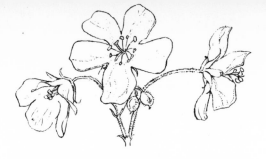

Geranium

Some flowers are named for heroes of myth and legend, some for scientists, some for their healing qualities. Not so the geranium, which is named for that long-legged, long-beaked wading bird, the crane. Its name is a translation of the old folk name "cranesbill" into botanists' Greek (*geranion* is the Greek for "crane"), and it is derived from the long beak of the plant's seed pods.

Somewhat confusingly, "geranium" can mean either of two flowers, the true geranium, which is best known as a wildflower, and the garden geranium, which botanists insist is not a geranium but a *pelargonium*.

Both flowers belong to the geranium family, and originally they were all called geraniums. In the late 1700's a French botanist named L'Heritier took a close look at the geraniums and decided that his scientist's conscience required him to divide them into *geraniums* (cranesbills), *pelargoniums* (storksbills, from the Greek *pelargos*, "stork"), and *erodiums* (heronsbills, from the Greek *erodios*, "heron"). And so the mischief was done, and ever since then pedantic flower lovers have sneered at those who called pelargoniums "geraniums." But any flower catalog will list them as geraniums, since that is what most people persist in calling them.

The true geraniums—about 260 species of them—grow in temperate regions around the world. Probably the most widespread and the best known is the wild geranium of North America, which is also native to Europe, Asia, and North Africa. In late spring its flowers turn patches of woodland and field into carpets of color. Pink or purple are the natural colors of the wild geranium, and men have developed cultivated varieties that are blue and violet. However, the cranesbill geranium is not raised nearly as widely as its cousin the pelargonium.

The pelargonium, a native of South Africa, was unknown to Europeans until the 1600's, when the Dutch planted a permanent settlement at the Cape of Good Hope. The great era of the pelargonium began in the reign of Queen Victoria, and it is still with us, for the pelargonium is one of the easiest flowers to grow, whether in a suburban garden or in a pot on the windowsill of a big-city apartment. It flowers reliably, and it needs little care. In fact, too much watering is bad for it, since it is a native of a rather dry region. In places where the climate is warm all year round, as in southern California, the common pelargonium grows into a six-foot shrub, and it is sometimes used for hedges.

The last group of the family, the erodiums, are practically all mountain dwellers, native to the Mediterranean area. A few species are sometimes raised in rock gardens.

The pelargonium has enough variations to write a book about. There is an ivylike species, which can be trained to climb on a support. There are varieties with red, white, and pink flowers. There are even species that are raised for their fragrant leaves, such as the rose geranium and the lemon geranium, whose foliage gives off a pleasant scent when rubbed gently. (Don't rub them too hard, or you'll mangle the leaf.) There are also peppermint, nutmeg, and apple geraniums. The common geranium is sometimes called the fish geranium because its leaves give off a fishy aroma. But then it is raised for its flowers, not its leaves.

In the early Middle Ages, one kind of cranesbill geranium was used in Iceland to make a blue-gray dye for warriors' cloaks, something like our modern Air Force blue. Except for that, there was little practical use for the cranesbills, though their juice was sometimes rubbed on wounds. But the pelargonium is quite important to the perfume industry, particularly for making scented soaps. Geranium (pelargonium) oil was formerly also used to bait traps for Japanese beetles, since they prefer it to any other scent. And sometimes—the flower must blush for shame—it is used to adulterate rose and lavender perfumes.

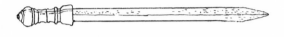

Gladiolus

Some 200 years ago, when Linnaeus was busily assigning names to plants, he gave the name *gladiolus* to a flower with long, pointed leaves that reminded him of a sword. *Gladiolus* is Latin for "little sword," and it derived from *gladius*, the sword with which the Roman legionaries conquered vast portions of Europe, North Africa, and the Near East. The *gladius*, a short, heavy sword with a sharp point and two cutting edges, could be used for both chopping and stabbing an enemy. In the hands of a trained Roman soldier, it was a deadly weapon.

From *gladius* also comes "gladiator." The gladiator was a professional sword fighter who performed in the public arena. If he won, a prize of money was his reward. If he lost, the winner put him to death for the pleasure of the crowd. However, Linnaeus was not trying to honor the cruel sport of gladiatorial combat. He was just a peaceful botanist writing in Latin, the international language of learned men.

The gladiolus belongs to the iris family, and its natural range stretches from the Mediterranean lands to South Africa. Most of the species come from the region around the Cape of Good Hope. About 1570 the English began to cultivate some of the European species, which they called "corn-flag." *Corn* was the general English word for "grain," and *flag* is an old name for the iris. Thus, corn-flag meant "grain-field iris," and in some places it was a troublesome pest in grain fields. Even in flower gardens, it had a tendency to spread insidiously and choke out other plants. The first of the South African glads reached England about 1660, and its bright red flowers made a hit.

At the time Shakespeare was writing his plays (late 1500's and early 1600's) medical men used a mash of gladiolus roots for drawing out splinters and thorns, while the dried seed pods, ground to powder and drunk with goat's or donkey's milk, were used as a remedy for colic.

The gladiolus was originally a much less showy flower than it is today—that is probably why Linnaeus noticed the leaves rather than the flowers. The modern types date from the 1840's, when a Belgian nurseryman made a lucky cross between varieties. Today gladioli range in color from white to deep shades of yellow, orange, and purple, and a red that is so deep it is almost black. There are even lime-green gladioli. There are so many shades of color that there is an official number code to designate them. Thus, the number 10 designates a light yellow gladiolus, and 42 designates a deep pink one. A similar code indicates the size of the blossoms, which may be anywhere from a little more than two inches to five and a half inches in diameter. Flowers between three and one-quarter to four and one-quarter inches are in the 300 category, under this system of classification. A gladiolus classified as 342, for example, would have flowers between three and one-quarter to four and one-quarter inches in diameter and be deep pink in color.

Growing gladioli (the Latin plural form) is a nationwide industry in the United States. In the Southern states thousands of acres of the flowers are harvested every winter and shipped to florists in northern cities. Thousands more acres in various Northern states produce them as a summer crop. Gladioli are most important as cut flowers for arrangements —for some reason they are often sent to people in hospitals and used for funeral decorations. They are also popular in gardens, where they are usually planted in the rear so as not to overshadow the other flowers.

Hibiscus

The name "hibiscus" suggests the blossom a South Sea maiden wears behind her ear as she waits for her true love in the moonlit, sweet-scented splendor of a tropic night on a wave-washed isle somewhere in the vastness of the Pacific. It is a romantic image, presented in a million bad movies and fifth-rate novels. But the real story of the hibiscus is far more than this.

To begin with, there are about 200 different species of hibiscus; they are native to warm parts of the world, mostly in Africa and Asia. A few are native to North America, and one or two are native to the islands of the Pacific. One of them is the state flower of Hawaii. The kinds that are most familiar in American gardens come from Africa, India, and China. It is believed that these cultivated varieties may have descended from plants that people raised for food two or three thousand years ago.

The hibiscus belongs to the mallow family. Its relatives include the hollyhock, the cotton plant, the various mallows, okra, and the familiar Rose of Sharon. The last two are true hibiscuses; the others are less closely related.

While most hibiscuses today are raised for their large, colorful flowers, some are raised for food. The okra plant is one of these. The edible part of okra is the seed pod, which is eaten when young and tender. The famous Louisiana dish called gumbo is based on okra. Okra probably originated in the wild highlands of Ethiopia and spread from there. In some countries okra is raised for its seeds, which yield a pretty good cooking oil. Sometimes okra seeds are ground and roasted as a substitute for coffee.

A few of the Asian hibiscuses are raised for their edible flower buds, which are used in curries and soups. Another species of hibiscus is grown in India for its fiber, which is used to make mats and coarse cloth.

"Hibiscus" comes from *hibiskos*, a Greek name for one of the mallow plants, and an old folk name for it is "rose mallow." Well before the Christian era, the Greeks and other peoples of the eastern Mediterranean were using mallows in medicine. The leaves, with their gooey juice, were used to soothe and soften rough skin and for a variety of other ailments. Three hundred years ago the Puritans of New England were still using mallows for skin lotion and to treat bee stings, constipation, pleurisy, head colds, sore throats, dandruff, baldness, and splinters. One wonders what a television commercial could do with mallows.

The marsh mallow was one of the mallows most prized for medicine, but it also gave its name to a sticky sweet. Marshmallows were originally made by cooking the roots of the plant with sugar. But the supply of marsh mallows could not meet the needs of the modern candy industry, and besides it was too expensive to gather the roots in the salt marshes where the mallows grew. Therefore, man's ingenuity had to supply what nature could not, and marshmallows are now made of sugar, corn starch, and corn syrup. Never having had a genuine marshmallow, I don't know what they tasted like, but they were probably even gooier than their modern namesakes.

Hollyhock

The hollyhock is no relation to the holly, despite its name. The name is misleading in more than one way, because it originally belonged to another plant, the marsh mallow. The Anglo-Saxons called the marsh mallow *holy hoc*: "holy" because they believed it had come from the Holy Land, and "hoc" being their name for mallow plants. Sometime around the middle 1500's the name "hollyhock" was shifted from the marsh mallow to the tall, flower-laden plant that we grow today. There is a story that the Crusaders brought it back to Europe from the Near East (this would account for the "holy"), but actually the hollyhock is a native of China. It is closely related to the marsh mallow, and the flowers look enough alike for the relationship to be recognized easily. But the marsh mallow is less than half the height of the hollyhock, which may grow to nine feet, and it does not bear such large flowers, or so many of them.

Like all the mallows, the hollyhock was used in medicine for many centuries. In fact, its scientific name, *Althaea*, comes from a Greek root meaning "to cure." (For the ways mallows were used in old-fashioned medicine, see the hibiscus entry.)

In the 1820's an Englishman whose name is now forgotten tried to raise hollyhocks on a gigantic scale, not for their flowers, but for the fiber of their stems, which he hoped would rival flax for making fine cloth and make him very rich. The experiment failed, which is why there are no hollyhock blouses or sport shirts today. While the hollyhock-farming project was going on, it was discovered that the plant yielded a blue dye equal in quality to indigo, which was then the best and most reliable blue dye known—and also very expensive. The English hollyhock promoter might have made a fortune if only the British textile makers had been willing to accept his dye. But whether the manufacturers were unwilling to take the risk of using a new product or whether the public refused to accept anything but the genuine indigo, he found no market for his hollyhock dye.

Honeysuckle

comes from the Anglo-Saxon *hunisuce,* from *hunig* ("honey")
plus *sucan* ("to suck"). Originally "honeysuckle" meant any
flower from which sweet nectar could be sucked—probably
by children, since grown-ups had no time for such un-
productive games. In parts of rural England this broad
meaning lingered on for hundreds of years. For example,
some country folk still call white clover blossoms "honeysuckle," or else remember that their grandparents did. However, by Shakespeare's time "honeysuckle" referred mainly
to a wild vine that bore great quantities of creamy-white

and red flowers, with a powerful sweet scent and full of nectar. Englishmen also called this plant "woodbine," from its habit of twining around trees and binding them.

There are about 180 species of honeysuckle, most of them native to North America or eastern Asia. However, enough parts of Europe had native honeysuckles to give the plant many different common names, such as honeysuckle, *madreselva* (Spanish, meaning "mother of the forest"), and a number of names meaning "goat leaf" in different languages, such as the French *chèvrefeuille* and the German *Geissblatt*. These names are translations of the Latin *caprifolium* (from *caper*, "goat," and *folium*, "leaf"), which was the name given to one species of honeysuckle by medieval herbalists. Was it named because goats loved to browse on the leaves? No, nothing so straightforward as that. It was because the plant climbed like a goat!

Not all honeysuckles climb. Some trail along the ground, and most species are bushes. Most honeysuckles bear colorful berries that birds are fond of eating, and conservationists recommend planting them to provide fall and winter food for birds. Bees and hummingbirds love the nectar-rich flowers.

In gardening, honeysuckle vines are used to screen porches and arbors and are trained along fences. Bush honeysuckles are used for hedges. Since most bush honeysuckles grow from eight to fifteen feet tall, they provide plenty of privacy (unless nosy neighbors climb up on the roof to keep tabs on you).

One species of honeysuckle that grows in Europe has very hard wood (its scientific name is Greek for "bone-wood"), and it was once used by country people to make teeth for rakes. Being hard, it did not wear out quickly, and the farm-workers did not have to spend their few moments of spare time replacing worn-out rake teeth.

The botanical name of the honeysuckle genus is *Lonicera*, after a sixteenth-century German physician and botanist, Adam Lonicer. One common honeysuckle vine, *Lonicera caprifolium*, gave its name to the whole honeysuckle family, or *Caprifoleaceae*. (In plant and animal classification, the family is the next larger group after *genus*, from a Latin word meaning "clan", and genus is the next larger group after *species*, Latin for "appearance" or "kind." All the species within the same genus are related and can interbreed; but species belonging to different genera in the same family are usually not related closely enough to interbreed.) The honeysuckle family includes a great number of ornamental flowering shrubs and also the elderberry bush, whose hollow stems country boys once made into whistles and blowguns, and whose small, purple-black berries their parents made into jelly and wine.

Although honeysuckle was not used in medicine, Scottish witches once used it for magical "cures" of sick persons, passing the patient nine times (a very magical number) through a wreath of green woodbine. Perhaps the underlying idea was that the woodbine would grip the demons causing the illness as tightly as it gripped the trees of the forest, while the green leaves stood for the flourishing health that the sick person was supposed to regain. If the patient believed strongly enough, the ritual might have made him feel better, at least for a time.

In Shakespeare's time the honeysuckle was a symbol of affection and faithfulness, because of its sweet scent and its habit of hugging tight to trees and supports. It was also used to cover bowers and garden walks, giving shelter from sun and rain, and incidentally creating a wonderful meeting place for lovers.

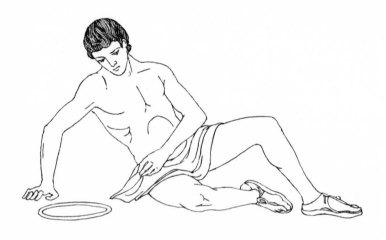

Hyacinth

The Greeks had a myth about a handsome youth named Hyakinthos, with whom both Apollo, the sun god, and Zephyros, the god of the west wind, fell in love. Their rivalry proved to be fatal to poor Hyakinthos, for he loved only Apollo. Vengefully brooding over his rejection, Zephyros waited for a chance to vent his spite. One day Apollo invited Hyakinthos to play a game of quoits with him. (A quoit is a flat, heavy ring of metal, and the object of the game is to throw it over a peg in the ground.) When Apollo tossed his quoit, Zephyros released a mighty blast of wind that flung the quoit like a deadly missile at Hyakinthos' head, killing him instantly. From the drops of his blood that fell to the ground there sprang up a dark-blue flower, bearing on its petals the letters *Ai! Ai!* (Woe! Woe!). The gods gave Hyakinthos' name to this flower so that he would live on in men's memories forever.

In this way the Greeks accounted for the origin of one of the flowers of their homeland, but the myth has a deeper meaning, and it is far older than the Greeks. It is told of many flowers in different lands around the Mediterranean. The people of the ancient Mediterranean civilizations lived by farming, and one of the most important happenings in their lives was the miraculous birth of vegetation in the spring, promising them grain for their daily bread and pasture for their flocks. To explain why the plants on which their lives depended came up fresh and green in the spring, died under the withering heat of the summer sun, and reappeared the next spring, they invented myths about gods and heroes who died, but even in dying gave birth to new life. Since the wildflowers were one of the first signs of the coming of spring, the season of life and growth, the ancient peoples associated them with their dying gods of plant life, and they became symbols in the myths. The story of Hyakinthos and Apollo is one such myth.

When the Romans conquered Greece, they found that the Greek myths were remarkably similar to their own, except that the gods had different names. So they took the Greek myths over wholesale, giving some of the gods the names of their Latin counterparts and changing others to suit the Latin pronunciation and spelling. Thus, Hyakinthos became Hyacinthus.

Many think that when Christianity became the official religion of the Roman Empire, the pagan Hyacinthus was transformed into Saint Hyacinthus, and children were named after him. Hyacinthe is a girls' name in France; Giacinto, the Italian version, is a man's name in Italy; and Jacinto is a man's name in Spain. There was also a Saint Hyacinthus in the thirteenth century who became famous as the Apostle to the Slavs. And people who have studied the Texan War of Independence against Mexico will remember that the final battle of that war was the Battle of San Jacinto.

The hyacinth of the ancient Greeks was almost certainly not the flower we call hyacinth today. Historians think it may have been a larkspur or an iris, or perhaps a dark-red lily. The modern hyacinth was originally a rather insignificant wildflower of the lily family, with small, dark-blue blossoms, looking rather like an unsuccessful bluebell. Native to the Near East, it seems to have been first cultivated in the botanical garden of the University of Padua, in Italy, around 1550. Padua was then one of Europe's leading medical schools, and the hyacinth was probably cultivated for possible use in medicine.

The flower was probably given the name hyacinth because of its color, for scholars generally agreed that the hyacinth of the Greek myth was blue. Indeed, a gemstone was also named hyacinth for its blue color. Some experts, however, insisted that "hyacinth" really meant red, orange, or amber-colored, and they combed the old Greek and Roman manuscripts to find statements that would bolster their arguments.

In cultivation the hyacinth developed more and brighter flowers than it had ever produced in the wild, and it became a popular garden flower. Before 1600, Englishmen were growing several varieties of hyacinth, which they sometimes spelled as *jacinth*. The greatest hyacinth growers, however, were the Dutch, who developed hundreds of new strains, with colors ranging from the original blue through white, pink, red, and purple, and many with mixed colors.

Thanks to the efforts of the Dutch growers, hyacinths became a frantically sought-after status symbol in the 1700's, and wealthy Englishmen were known to pay as much as 200 pounds for a single bulb of a particularly prized variety. (That sum was expected to provide a comfortable living for several years for a country parson and a large family, and it was more than an ordinary workman could earn in a lifetime.) Naturally the Dutch growers went to fantastic lengths to safeguard such a source of wealth. They circulated rumors that Dutch hyacinth bulbs were so delicate that they would flower only once and then had to be replaced by fresh bulbs. This was not true, but for nearly a century they were successful in deceiving foreign gardeners.

New strains, of course, were particularly valuable, and there is a story that the Dutchman who created the first lilac-flowered hyacinth kept the plant in a birdcage hung from his ceiling, for fear that mice would somehow get at it and devour it. The scheme worked; the ravenous rodents were held at bay; and the plant survived to have millions of descendants.

Iris

The Greeks had a god or goddess for almost every conceivable purpose, and Iris was the goddess of the rainbow. She was Juno's attendant and a messenger for the gods. The rainbow, said the Greek myth spinners, was a bridge down which she sped to carry messages to the earth. Her duties also included guiding the souls of dead women to the Elysian Fields, the ancient Greek counterpart of heaven. In this belief the Greeks often planted irises on the graves of women, for the flower was sacred to her.

Irises grow wild over much of the eastern Mediterranean region, including the craggy peninsulas and islands of Greece. Some are yellow, suggesting the sun; some are blue, suggesting the sky. Perhaps the sunny yellow and sky blue of the flowers led the Greeks to associate them with the sky goddess Iris and name them for her; or perhaps they did so because the flowers are often striped, which may have suggested the rainbow's stripes.

Man and the iris have been together for thousands of years. Archeologists found irises painted on the walls of the great palace of Knossos on ⌐ which was built around 2500 B.C. About 1450 P ⌐ ⌐ Pharaoh, Thutmose III, brought irises ba ⌐ the territories he had conquered in the Near East. He planted them in his palace garden as a symbol of his triumph. To make certain that his feats would not be forgotten, he had the flowers carved on the wall of the temple of Amen, the sun god.

As a sacred flower the iris was credited with healing powers, and it was much used in ancient medicine. In the first century A.D. a Greek physician named Dioscorides wrote a book in which he summed up all that was then known about medicinal plants. The iris led his list. Dioscorides probably served as a doctor with the armies of the Roman emperor Nero, and he had a great deal of practical knowledge. His book, *De Materia Medica* (*About the Materials of Medicine*), contained many useful facts along with the superstition and unrealistic theory that then passed for knowledge. It remained one of the standard medical works for nearly 1,900 years.

Dioscorides recommended iris root, drunk with honey, vinegar, or wine, for coughs, colds, indigestion, and sciatica. He said it was good as a poultice for tumors and ulcers, broken bones, and headache. Mixed with honey and hellebore, the roots would also remove freckles and sunburn. People of ancient times considered freckles and sunburn highly undesirable. A pale complexion was held up as the ideal of beauty. To be sunburned meant that you were a peasant, who had to work outdoors, and were thus at the bottom of the social scale. And since our notions of beauty have always been tied up with social snobbery, anything connected with the wrong class has automatically been ugly. Not until the late 1800's, when most people worked in factories and never saw the sun, did pallor become unfashionable and a good suntan the badge of privilege.

Thanks to Dioscorides, iris was raised in medicinal herb gardens even after the Roman empire fell, and it remained a mainstay of herbal medicine down through the time when the Puritans settled in New England. In fact, irises actually do have genuine medical qualities, though nothing like what Dioscorides and other ancient writers claimed for them. As late as 1938 they were listed in the US Pharmacopoeia, the official list of approved drugs, though they have now been replaced by more effective remedies.

Irises had many uses outside of medicine. In Germany the fragrant roots of one species, known as orris root, were hung in barrels of beer to keep it from going stale. In France orris roots ("orris" is a corruption of "iris") were used to enrich the aroma of wine, which would surely horrify a modern wine expert. In England they were used to flavor brandy. Today orris root is used to flavor toothpaste. It is also one of the main sources of violet perfume, for the chemical substance that gives orris root its fragrance is identical to that of violets.

More yet: Iris seeds can be ground and used as a coffee substitute (probably not a very good one); Belgian artists used to make a green pigment from the flowers; Scottish Highlanders made ink from the roots; and the leaves served as emergency rations for cattle. French peasant women used to boil orris root with the wash to make their clothes fragrant.

The iris belongs to the iris family. There are about 1,200 species of iris growing wild around the world, all in temperate regions north of the equator. It is Tennessee's state flower. With such a wide distribution, the iris acquired many local names, most of which are now too obscure and obsolete to be mentioned here. One that is still used, however, is "flag." This name comes from a Germanic word of obscure origin—even the dictionary makers cannot puzzle it out—and it originally meant any plant with long, swordlike leaves that grew in bogs. Eventually its meaning narrowed down to the "sweet flag," a rush with a sweet-smelling root, and the "yellow flag," a yellow iris that grows in wet spots all over Europe and the Near East. Later the name was also given to blue irises, which sensibly enough are called "blue flags."

The French call the iris *fleur-de-lis*. For centuries the fleur-de-lis was the emblem of the French kings, and it is still as much a French symbol as the eagle is American. There are many legends as to how the fleur-de-lis became a royal symbol and how it got its name. They begin with Clovis, king of the Franks (466?–511 A.D.). The Franks were a rather barbaric German tribe who hacked their way through the Roman border outposts and with sword, spear, and battle-ax established themselves as rulers of a large part of present-day France. They also gave their name to the country: "France" is just a softened version of *Frankia*.

Clovis was a pagan, but his wife was a Christian. According to one legend, he promised to become a Christian if the Christian god would help him in battle against his enemies. God granted him victory, and he was converted. In honor of both events he replaced the three toads on his chieftain's banner with three iris flowers, for the iris was sacred to the Virgin Mary.

Another legend says that Clovis and his warriors were getting the worst of a battle with the Goths, another powerful Germanic tribe. With their backs to a wide river and a tireless foe facing them, things looked very bad—until Clovis noticed that a bed of yellow iris was growing all the way across the river. Realizing that this must mean the water was shallow enough to ford, Clovis led his army to safety. In gratitude he took the flower for his emblem.

A different story gives the credit to a French king named Louis VII, who ruled about 600 years after Clovis. An extremely pious man, Louis organized a crusade, which was a disastrous failure. For his emblem he chose three purple irises, which he said had been revealed to him in a holy dream. At any rate, Louis did have three fleur-de-lis as his emblem, and many language historians think that "fleur-de-lis" was originally *fleur de Louis*, or "flower of Louis." Since Louis usually spelled his name "Loys," this theory may be right. The name could have gone through the stages of *fleur-de-Loys, fleur-de-lys*, and the present spelling of *fleur-de-lis*. The English managed to twist it into "flower-de-luce" and "flordelice," but both these variations have withered away like spent flowers.

The fleur-de-lis symbol has also been traced to a lily (*lis* is the French word for "lily"), a sword, and a spearhead. Take your choice. It would be difficult to prove you are wrong.

Lilac

The lilac has for centuries been one of the most popular flowering shrubs, as much for the fragrance of its big flower clusters as for their color. The lilac is native to a huge territory extending from eastern Europe to Japan. The common lilac of gardens and dooryards comes from eastern Europe, but its name comes from farther east, in Persia.

The Persians raised lilacs in their walled pleasure gardens and called them *nilak*, meaning "bluish," for the color of their flowers. *Nilak* comes from *nil*, an ancient Indo-European word for the dark-blue color of indigo. Some Persians perversely said *lilak* instead of *nilak*, and this form was picked up by their Moslem neighbors, the Arabs. From the Arabs the name passed on to their old enemies the Spaniards, who spelled it with a "c" because they do not use the letter "k" in their alphabet. The French adopted the name *lilac* from the Spaniards, and it was in this form that it entered the English language about 1625. (In modern French it is *lilas.*) The plant itself was known long before then, and English gardeners called it "pipe-tree" or "blue pipe-privet."

The lilac is related to the privet, an evergreen hedge plant, for both of them belong to the olive family. Its scientific name, *Syringa*, comes from the Greek *syrinx*, a tube or pipe, which was originally used for the musical instrument known as the Pan-pipe. In the crabbed mixture of classical languages spoken by medieval scholars, this became *syringa*. This was the word chosen by a sixteenth-century French botanist named Mathieu L'Obel for a bush whose hollow shoots were used for the stems of tobacco pipes. The plant L'Obel meant was the mock-orange, but in 1753 Linnaeus appropriated the name *syringa* for the lilac. Since L'Obel had been dead more than a hundred years, he was in no condition to make objections, and Linnaeus tried to make up for his action by naming a lovely flower *Lobelia* in his honor.

It is said that the first cultivated lilacs were brought to Europe from Constantinople (now Istanbul, Turkey) in 1554. The Turks pronounced the name as *leylaq*, and this passed into English as "laylock," a form that is no longer used.

112

The original Persian lilacs from which the name was derived were a light purplish-blue in color, and this is what "lilac" as a color means today. But centuries of cultivation have given us lilacs that are deep purple, crimson, light blue, dark blue, pink, white, and yellow as well. The lilac plant itself is a woody shrub. Depending on the variety, it ranges from 4 to 10 feet tall, or even taller with good growing conditions. Like forsythias, lilacs send up many shoots from their roots, so that in a few years a small bush can turn into a tall thicket. As they grow old, lilac bushes become quite gnarled and picturesque.

The Englishmen who settled in New England were fond of lilacs, and after they had gotten established they imported them from the old country. They were one of the

commonest dooryard plants of New England farmhouses, and gnarled old lilac bushes can still be found blooming in the ruins of abandoned farms. In recognition of this old New England tradition, the lilac was made the state flower of New Hampshire. It is also the state flower of Idaho, though not many New Englanders settled there.

Lily

The lily family is a very large one. It includes many ornamental flowers, plus asparagus, onions, garlic, chives, squill (used for rat poison), the spiny aloe, smilax—better known as cat briar, the vegetable equivalent of barbed wire—and the gigantic dragon's-blood tree of the Canary Islands. But it is the lilies themselves we are interested in here.

"Lily" comes from the Anglo-Saxon *lilie*, which is adapted

from the Latin *lilium*. The Latin name probably comes from *leirion*, the Greek name for the lily, and language scholars have not been able to trace the word further back. Most of the European names for the flower come from the Latin or Greek names, such as *Lilie* (German), *lely* (Dutch), *lilja* (Swedish), and *lirio* (Spanish). Some are a little bit difficult to recognize, such as *lis* (French), and *giglio* (Italian, and pronounced jeel-yo).

Lilies have a very long history. White lilies were sacred to the great goddess of ancient Crete, where a mighty civilization flourished as long ago as 3,000 B.C. The Cretans also decorated the walls of their palaces and houses with paintings of dark-red lilies, the kind the Greeks called *krinon*. The Greeks, who inherited much of their culture from Crete, made the white lily sacred to Hera, their chief goddess, and the Romans held it sacred to Juno. In Christian tradition the white lily, a symbol of purity, is sacred to the Virgin Mary.

Only three flowers are mentioned by name in the Old Testament of the Bible. The lily is one of them. The Hebrew name for the lily is *shoshan* or *shoshannah*, from which come the familiar names Susan and Susannah. Lily and Lilian, too, are girls' names in many countries.

In ancient times the name "lily" must have been used for flowers in general. For instance, the lilies of the field mentioned in the Bible are thought to have been narcissus, white lilylike flowers of the amaryllis family, or even anemones, which don't look like lilies at all. Even today "lily" is still used for some flowers that are not related to the lily, such as the water lily, which belongs to the lotus family, and the calla lily, which belongs to the arum family and is related to jack-in-the-pulpit and skunk cabbage.

Lilies grow all around the northern hemisphere, and they have adapted to almost every kind of environment, from meadows high in the mountains to lowlands; from hot, dry semideserts, as in the Near East, to cool North American forests and bogs. They are white, red, pink, purple, yellow, orange—in fact, almost every color except blue. Many lilies are spotted or striped. These markings may have evolved to help bees and other insects that pollinate the flowers detect them more easily.

One of the best-known spotted lilies is the tiger lily, whose orange-red or brick-red petals are speckled with black spots. Native to the Far East, the tiger lily was intro-

duced to the West in 1804, when an English botanist sent some home to London, but it has been raised for more than a thousand years in China, Japan, and Korea. Actually it was raised more as a vegetable than a flower, for the people of these countries ate the bulbs.

It must have been a Chinese poet who gave the tiger lily its name, for orange-red tigers with black dots instead of stripes are not easy to find, even in China. The Japanese, who have no tigers of any color, call it the Ogre Lily.

White lilies were much used in old-time medicine. Queen Elizabeth's physician prescribed the juice of the bulbs, mixed with barley flour and baked into bread, to treat dropsy. It was believed that the bulbs, mashed up with honey, would knit together sinews, heal burns without a scar, and restore hair to bald spots. The same lily-and-honey mixture was said to clear up pimply complexions and remove wrinkles. The ancient Romans used a poultice of the bulbs to treat corns.

Modern science has proven all these lily remedies to be worthless, and one wonders why people continued to use them for so many centuries. Perhaps faith in the words of the revered authorities, mingled with superstition and belief in magic, played a part. Or perhaps the patients took comfort in the thought that they might have felt even worse without the medicines.

Two well-known "lilies," the day lily and the lily of the valley, are not true lilies, but they do belong to the lily family. The day lily is named for the fact that its flowers last only for a day. Its scientific name, *Hemerocallis*, is Greek for "beautiful for a day."

Native from eastern Europe to China, day lilies were brought to the United States to decorate gardens with their masses of brilliant orange and yellow flowers, but they soon escaped from cultivation and now grow wild. The Chinese, who rank among the world's great cooks, use the buds and flowers of day lilies as vegetables.

The lily of the valley is native to Europe, eastern Asia, and North America. Its name is an English translation of the Latin *lilium convallarium* (*convallis* is the Latin term for a valley shut in by hills, and *lilium*, as you will remember, means "lily"). The Old Testament mentions a flower called "lily of the valleys" (in Hebrew, *shoshan ha-amakim*), and this became *lilium convallarium* when the Bible was first translated into Latin. However, it is pretty certain that the Hebrew lily of the valley was not the same as the flower we know, for the lily of the valley needs a cool, moist, shady spot to grow in, and such places were scarce in the land of Israel. But the name became attached to the plant with the tiny, sweet-smelling, bell-shaped white flowers, perhaps because it had been sacred to some of the pagan gods of Europe. In Norse mythology it was the special flower of the dawn goddess. The scientific name of the lily of the valley, *Convallaria majalis*, refers to its habit of blooming in May (*majalis* is Latin for "of May").

There are many legends about the lily of the valley. One of the best-known tells how the devil, disguised as a dragon, battled a saint named Leonard. As Leonard chased the dragon through the forest, it clawed and bit him, wounding him severely. In every spot where the saint's blood fell on the ground, a patch of lilies of the valley sprang up. A Norse legend tells how the goddess of spring woke up and saw nothing around her but bleak, barren rocks and patches of snow. She was so distressed by the ugly sight that she tore up her green dress to make leaves and made the white flowers from a handful of snow.

In Ireland people called lily of the valley "fairy ladders," for they believed that fairies ran up and down the stems, jumping from blossom to blossom. English country people called them wood lilies and May lilies. Another old name was "mugget," from *muguet,* the French name for the flower. The name "Our Lady's Tears" came from a legend that the flowers sprang from the Virgin Mary's tears at the death of Jesus.

The lily of the valley had many uses in medicine. It was used as a lotion for sore hands, gout, sprains, bad complexion, and eye inflammations. Distilled with wine, the flowers were used for dumb palsy, apoplexy, leprosy, vertigo, and heart trouble. In using lily of the valley for heart trouble, the old-time herbalists were on good ground. The plant contains a poisonous substance, which, in very small doses, stimulates the heart muscle. Modern doctors sometimes prescribe this drug for heart patients instead of digitalis.

The water lily is no relation to the lilies, for it belongs to the lotus family. It grows wild all around the northern hemisphere. The familiar water lily of the United States is yellow, but there are also white water lilies, and in Sweden there are red ones.

The yellow water lily has such folk names as pond lily, cow lily, and spatterdock. North American Indians used it for food. They also made a tea from the roots as a remedy for diarrhea. White settlers in New England copied this remedy from the Indians and found it useful.

The water lily helped the Indians in more than one way. Moose relish water lilies, and they wade far out in the water to reach them, dipping their heads under water to get at the succulent roots. In this position they made an easy target for Indian hunters, and the tribe could eat well.

Although the true lily has many sacred associations, its name has been linked with some evil superstitions, and it has also been used as an insult. Witches used lilies in a preparation to give someone a fever or dry up the milk of his cows. To dream of white lilies could foretell your death, for lilies were a flower of the dead. The Hungarians used to say that three yellow lilies would spring up on the spot where an innocent person had been executed. "Lily-livered" means cowardly, and it was a favorite insult in times gone by. It had to be used with caution, however, for the person you accused of owning a lily liver might try to defend his reputation by punching you in the nose.

Lotus

comes from *lotos*, the name given by the Greeks to a magical plant in the great poem the *Odyssey*. By a remarkable process of confusion, it refers today to at least four different plants: the Egyptian lotus, the sacred lotus of India, the lotus of botanists, and the plant referred to by the Greeks.

The Egyptian lotus is native to Egypt and the lakes and streams of Central Africa. A member of the water-lily family, it grows in great abundance in the Nile River, whose

valley was the heartland of the ancient Egyptian civilization.

The lotus was an important religious symbol to the Egyptians. To them it symbolized the sun, perhaps because of its raylike petals and because the blossoms open in the morning and close in the evening, as the sun rises and sets. The sun god was particularly important in Egyptian religion. One of the many myths about the birth of the sun god tells how, in the beginning, the world was covered by water. But a lotus grew up to the surface of the primeval sea and unfolded its leaves and buds in the air. A flower opened up, and the infant sun god appeared miraculously among its petals. (This was an important theme in several ancient religious.)

There are white and blue Egyptian lotuses, and the people of ancient Egypt were fond of both. They used them for garlands and decorations, and the wealthy grew them in pools in their gardens. The lotus was one of the chief emblems in Egyptian art. It was used in tomb paintings more than 4,000 years ago, and skilled stone-cutters carved the tops of temple columns to look like graceful clusters of lotus buds. In fact, the lotus remained a popular motif in jewelry, pottery, and architecture down to the beginning of the Christian Era.

The lotus is also mentioned in the writings of Herodotus, a Greek who visited Egypt in the fifth century B.C. Herodotus, who is often called "the father of history," was the first great travel writer. He visited many different lands and wrote vivid descriptions of the people and their strange (to him) customs. He also repeated many fantastic and untrue fables for the amusement of his sensation-hungry and credulous fellow Greeks, such as yearly battles between pigmies and cranes, giant ants of India that mined and hoarded gold, and strange races of men with faces like dogs, or with bodies consisting only of a head and one gigantic foot. However, in these cases he was careful to state that he was only passing along stories that others had told him. When it came to the things he had seen for himself, he was an honest and sharp-eyed reporter. While Herodotus said nothing about the lotus as a sacred emblem, he did report that the Egyptians ate the roots of a kind of water lily they called *lotus*, and that the roots were round, sweet, and about the size of an apple. They also dried the lotus blossoms and ground them into flour for bread.

It would seem from Herodotus' description that *lotus* was the native Egyptian name for the plant. Its modern botanical name is *Nymphaea lotus*. In Greek mythology the nymphs were spirits, usually described as beautiful young women who lived in the water, so the name was a good choice for a beautiful water plant.

The sacred lotus of India has been cultivated since prehistoric times for its edible roots and nutlike seeds. It is still used in Oriental cooking. A member of the water-lily family, it is related to the Egyptian lotus. Botanists think that the sacred lotus originated in southeastern Asia and that wandering tribes carried it to India and China in very ancient times. If archeological evidence means anything, the sacred lotus became a religious symbol nearly 5,000 years ago, for a crude figure of a fertility goddess unearthed from a ruined city in northwestern India had a lotus blossom in its hair.

Perhaps it was the importance of the lotus as food that first led Asians to regard it as sacred, but as the cultures of Asia evolved, many more meanings were added to its symbolism. The lotus came to stand not only for fertility but for life, happiness and prosperity, death and resurrection, immortality, the earth and its creation, the sun, spiritual power, wisdom, and purity.

The lotus appears in many Hindu legends. Like the Egyptian sun god, many of the Hindu gods were said to have been born miraculously in a lotus flower. (The Hindu and Egyptian legends were created independently, however. There is no evidence that either ancient civilization even knew of the other.) In Indian poetry the lotus was the ultimate expression of all that was beautiful, and goddesses were described as lotus-eyed or having complexions like the lotus.

The lotus is one of the basic symbols of Buddhism, and
Buddha is usually shown seated on a lotus, his feet folded
under him in the famous lotus posture of meditation. Buddha was raised as a Hindu; and when he founded his re-
formed faith, he kept many Hindu ideas and symbols, including the lotus. After his death his followers told many of
the old myths of the Hindu gods about him. In one myth
lotuses sprang out of the ground at every step he took. In
one of the Buddhist versions of paradise the souls of the
dead rest in lotus blossoms on a sacred lake.

The sacred lotus now grows in Egypt, too, although it is
not native there. It seems to have been brought in as a food
plant by the Romans, who conquered Egypt in the first century B.C. It probably received the name "lotus" then, from
its resemblance to the Egyptian lotus. The Indian name of

the sacred lotus is *padma*. The famous Buddhist prayer, *"Om mani padme hum,"* means "Oh! The jewel in the lotus!" (The jewel stands for the soul of the individual, and the lotus stands for the divine universe—at least in one of the many interpretations of the prayer.) The botanical name of the sacred lotus is *Nelumbo*, taken from a native Ceylonese name for the flower.

The lotus of botanists is a group of plants belonging to the pea family. Most of them are cloverlike; some are pealike trailing vines; and a few are small shrubs. It is difficult to think of any good reason why botanists should have used the ancient and recognized name of the water-dwelling lotus for these unrelated dry-land plants.

The famous *lotos* of Greek mythology is a spiny shrub or small tree native to North Africa, southern Europe, and southern Asia. It bears a fruit that has been variously described as resembling a date or a small plum. The lotus fruit, although sweetish, is dry and mealy inside; so it is usually made into bread or fermented into a kind of beer rather than eaten fresh. It was a traditional food of poor people—the more fortunate passed it up in favor of something better tasting.

This lotus is also known as *jujube*, a medieval Latin perversion of *zizafun*, the Arabic name of the fruit. Middle Eastern peoples also made a candy of the fruit, mashed and sweetened to improve the flavor. In the nineteenth century, when European powers were busy carving out empires in the Middle East, jujube candies became popular in Europe and the United States. Something like a gumdrop, they are still eaten today, but they are now made from such rare and costly ingredients as gelatin, corn syrup, and artificial flavoring, not from the fruit of the legendary lotus tree.

Apparently the lotus tree was not as widely distributed in ancient Greek times as it is today, for the Greek poet Homer described it as something unknown to the Greeks. In the *Odyssey* he told how Odysseus, returning home to Greece after the conquest of Troy, was blown far off his course by a storm sent by angry gods. After nine storm-tossed days, during which they did not know if they would survive, Odysseus and his men landed in a sheltered harbor in Libya. There they were welcomed by the inhabitants, a tribe known as the Lotos Eaters. These people lived on the enchantingly sweet and refreshing fruits of the lotus tree, and they generously offered some to the hungry Greeks, who ate them with relish. Then a strange thing happened. The Greeks lost all desire to see their homeland again, and they told Odysseus that all they wanted to do was lie around and eat lotus fruits. They even began to forget where they came from. Odysseus had to force them back to the ship at sword's point to continue the voyage.

Homer explained this as the work of enchantment. But what could have been more natural for the Greek sailors, exhausted after their near-fatal experience in the storm, and terrified of running into more perils on the sea, than to choose to stay safe and well fed on land and forget about going home? Even if they had to live on such poor food as lotus fruits, which Homer described with the deceitful skill of a modern advertising man.

Marigold

was originally "Mary's gold"—Mary being the Virgin Mary and gold referring to the color of the flower. The Virgin must have been well supplied with golden flowers, for the name has been used for at least four different ones.

As far back as the 1200's, English writers frequently mentioned a flower they called the "golde" or "Mary golde." They could have meant the corn marigold, a kind of chrysanthemum, or the marsh marigold, which belongs to the buttercup family. But if they were writing about cooking or medicine, it was almost certainly the calendula they meant. The flower we now know as the marigold is a native of Mexico and did not reach Europe until the 1500's.

130

The calendula (both its scientific name and its common name) is native to southern Europe. The Romans cultivated it both as a flower and as a medicinal plant, and its name comes from the Latin word *calendae*, which was the Roman term for the first days of each month. (Our word "calendar" comes from the same root.) Historians think the calendula was named because it was believed to bloom at the beginning of each month. In places with mild climates this may have been true.

Europeans used the calendula marigold for fever remedies and also made it into a jam that was supposed to relieve heart palpitations. But more than anything else they esteemed it as a kitchen herb. Calendula blossoms were in great demand for flavoring soup; indeed, they were used for this purpose down into the 1800's. One English traveler around 1600 told of seeing barrels full of calendula blossoms in grocery shops in the Netherlands. This "marigold" was also used for flavoring puddings, dumplings, and porridge. Wine was made from the petals.

The calendula folds its petals together when the sun goes down and opens up again in the morning. Many writers in the reign of Queen Elizabeth were fascinated by this behavior, and Shakespeare composed a poetic line about "the marigold that goes to bed with the sun/And with him rises weeping." (The tears of the marigold were drops of dew on the petals.)

The corn marigold was not nearly so important a flower as the calendula. In fact, it seems to have been known chiefly as a weed in grain fields. It is grown to some extent today as a garden flower. Like the calendula, it belongs to the *Compositae* family.

The marsh marigold looks rather like a giant version of its little cousin the buttercup. Another name for it is "kingcup." Around 1600, Europeans took this wildflower into their gardens and began cultivating it, with spectacular results. In the same period, the marsh marigold was used to treat anemia and epilepsy, but cautious physicians advised against taking the flowers into a young girl's room, "lest she be liable to fits of madness." Country people in New England used to eat young marsh marigold leaves as spring greens, getting some badly needed vitamins at the end of the winter. The buds, it is said, can be pickled and eaten like capers.

The scientific name of the marsh marigold is *Caltha palustris*, from the Greek *kalthos*, "cup" (referring to the shape of the flowers, which look like small golden bowls an inch across), and the Latin *palustris*, "of the swamp" (from *palus*, "swamp," and referring to the kind of place where the flower likes to grow).

The current holder of the title "marigold" is distantly related to the calendula and the corn marigold. Its scientific

name is *Tagetes*, which is derived from the name of an Etruscan god, Tages, who was famous for his beauty. This marigold is native to Mexico and South America, and the Aztecs, who loved bright-colored flowers, raised it both as an ornamental flower and as a kitchen herb. Despite its birthplace, this flower used to be known as the French marigold and the African marigold.

Seeds of the "African" marigold had been taken to Spain from the New World not long after 1500, and the flower had become popular there. Some seeds must have blown across to North Africa, because by 1535 marigolds were growing wild there. In that year the soldiers of a Spanish expedition against the Moors in North Africa thought the marigolds were native North African plants and brought some home to Spain as mementoes, naming them after the place they had taken them from.

The "French" marigold, a smaller species than the "African" marigold, was supposedly brought to England by Protestant refugees from France about 1570, hence its name.

Many people dislike the strong scent of the marigold; one English writer about 1600 went so far as to say, "Its smell is hateful, nay I should rather say, injurious." Some people even concluded that any flower with such a smell must obviously be poisonous, and one old-time writer claimed that when he fed a cat marigold blossoms mixed with cheese, the cat swelled up and died most horribly.

Scent and stories notwithstanding, the marigold became a popular garden flower in both Europe and the United States. One marigold fancier, a Senator from Illinois, tried for years to have the marigold declared the national flower of the United States. One of the aims of marigold fanciers is to breed unusual varieties, and for years they have been attempting to create a white marigold. Some of the big seed-growing companies have long offered a reward to anyone who can grow a pure white marigold. No one has yet succeeded, although there are now some very, very pale yellow varieties.

In its ancient homeland of Mexico the marigold has one of the most surprising uses a flower could have. Hundreds of acres of bright-orange marigolds are raised so that the flowers can be dried, powdered, and fed to chickens to make them lay eggs with healthy-looking orange yolks. Most of the product goes to the big egg producers of the United States. If your breakfast egg looked especially appetizing, thank the marigolds.

Narcissus

is named from a Greek myth which tells a story of callous vanity and its well-deserved punishment.

Narcissus was the son of a river god and a nymph. He was so unbelievably handsome that women and men alike were continually falling in love with him. But Narcissus was as vain and self-centered as he was handsome, and he coldly rejected all those who asked for his love, for he was sure that he was far too good for any of them. By the time he was sixteen, he had left a trail of hundreds of broken hearts behind him, but he did not feel the least bit of sympathy.

One of the luckless ones who fell in love with Narcissus was Echo, a nymph. Echo was a comely and delightful young maiden with only one fault: She always had to have the last word. One day she fell afoul of Hera, chief of the female gods of Olympus. Hera was hot on the trail of her faithless husband, Zeus, who she suspected was disporting himself with some young nymphs while she was busy with

the work of the divine household. Echo, loyal to her sister
nymphs, distracted Hera with idle chatter while they made
their escape. Cheated of her vengeance, Hera punished
Echo cruelly, telling her, "You'll always have the last word
from now on, but you'll never have the first!"

From that moment, Echo was unable to utter any words
but the last words someone else had just said. The other
nymphs soon had enough of this tiresome new habit of
Echo's and drove her away. She wandered by herself in the
woods, until one day she spied Narcissus out hunting, and
she fell hopelessly in love with him. Unable to express her
love in words, she ran up to embrace him, repeating the tag

136

ends of everything he said. Narcissus rebuffed her haughtily, vowing that he would die before he ever had anything to do with her. Crushed by this heartless rejection, Echo hid in lonely glens, pining away in misery until only her voice was left.

This did not bother Narcissus in the slightest, for he cared for no one but himself. He went on as before, callous and conceited. When a river god named Ameinius fell in love with him, Narcissus sent him a sword. Ameinius took the hint and killed himself, calling on the gods to avenge his death. Artemis, the goddess of hunting, heard his plea and resolved that Narcissus must be punished.

Her punishment was cunningly contrived. Narcissus' favorite pastime was hunting, so she magically led him on a long chase into a lonely clearing in the forest. In the center of the glade was a pool of crystal-clear water. Tired and hot and thirsty after his long chase, Narcissus flung himself down by the pool to get a cooling drink. As he did so, he saw the face of an unbelievably handsome youth. Narcissus did not quite understand who this beautiful stranger was, but he knew that he was instantly in love with him. He spoke to the other and saw his lips move as if in reply, but he heard no words returning his love. He bent down to kiss the handsome youth, but his lips met only chilly water. Time and again he tried to reach the young man in the pool, or at least speak with him, but each time he failed. At last he realized that the youth he had fallen in love with was his own reflection, and he could never possess him. Now experiencing the same rejection he had inflicted on so many others, Narcissus in a frenzy of frustration stabbed himself in the heart and expired. Where Narcissus' blood fell on the ground, a white flower with a red cup in its center sprang up. The gods gave it Narcissus' name so that it might serve as a warning to mortals.

In versions of the myth tailored for children and squeamish adults, Narcissus either drowned himself or pined away as Echo had. But the version given here is probably the oldest one, and some scholars think it hints darkly at bloody rites in which a handsome young man was sacrificed so that his blood would make the earth bring forth bountiful crops.

The name "narcissus" may come from the same root as "narcotic" (*narke*, meaning "numb"), and the Greeks prepared a pain-relieving drug from the plant. However, this drug was not used after the beginning of the Christian era, which was just as well, since the narcissus contains a dangerous poison. In modern times the myth of Narcissus added a new word to the language of medicine. In the 1920's psychiatrists coined the term "narcissism" to denote a condition of unhealthy self-love.

Botanically the narcissus is a member of the amaryllis family. It probably originated in Spain, since that is where the greatest number of wild species have been found, and spread from there all around the Mediterranean region, westward to Britain, and east to China and Japan. The narcissus came to America when the frontier period was past and people could afford the luxury of flowers that were of no use for food or medicine.

There are probably twenty-five or thirty species of narcissus and hundreds of garden varieties. Their petals may be yellow or white, and the crown in the center ranges from red-orange to palest yellow. The crown ranges in shape from a short cup to a long trumpet.

The ancient Greeks and Egyptians used narcissus for funeral wreaths, for the flower was associated with death. Its narcotic qualities may have suggested the long sleep of death, while its habit of blooming faithfully year after year in the spring may have symbolized the resurrection of the dead. In many cultures the narcissus is not a symbol of death, but of spring and the rebirth of life. In the Scandinavian countries it is an Easter symbol, and its popular name means "Easter lily."

An old favorite type of narcissus is the jonquil. Properly speaking, the name "jonquil" refers to a very fragrant, all-yellow species of narcissus with long, narrow leaves. The name comes from the Latin word *jonquilla*, meaning "little rush." (*Juncus* is Latin for "rush.") But the ancient Romans never spoke of *jonquillae*, for the word was made up by seventeenth-century French scholars as a more dignified version of the French folk-name *jonquille*, which refers to the plant's rushlike leaves. The jonquil was originally native to southern Europe and Algeria, but now it is grown in many parts of the world.

Another very popular type of narcissus is the daffodil. Botanically, "daffodil" refers to one or two species of narcissus with long, trumpetlike centers. In fact, one of them is also called "trumpet narcissus." However, many people use the name to mean all narcissi. Some botanists and dictionary makers smile kindly on this broad use of the name; others are sternly set against it. Whichever side you choose, you can take comfort in the fact that the argument has been going on for hundreds of years.

Nasturtium

The Romans relished a certain flowering plant whose juicy, green leaves added pungency to their salads. They called it *nasturtium*—freely translated, it means "nose twister"—from *nasus*, "nose," plus *tortus*, "twisted." (Our word "torture," by the way, comes from the same root as *tortus*.) A famous Roman writer, Pliny, claimed that the plant got its name from "the torment of the nostrils" when someone bit into the peppery-hot leaves.

The name *nasturtium* in Roman times and for centuries after meant the watercress and its relatives, which were raised as food plants. They were certainly not raised for their flowers, which are rather insignificant and not long lasting. But in the 1500's the name was given to a completely unrelated plant with spectacular flowers in glowing shades of orange, yellow, and red. A Spanish doctor named Nicolas Monardes played a part in the story, as he also did with the flower called nicotiana.

Monardes was always on the lookout for new plants that might have medicinal value, and he collected all kinds of plants and seeds that the Conquistadors brought home to Spain from the New World. From one batch of seeds from Peru, which looked rather like little balls of cork, he got plants with round leaves like a giant watercress and bright golden flowers shaped like the helmets worn by ancient Greek warriors. The leaves had a peppery taste like that of watercress, and so the new plant found its way into Europe's salads. Because of its resemblance to watercress in taste and the shape of the leaves, the old name of nasturtium was given to the new plant from the far-off realm of the Incas. Some people called it "Indian cress," a name that is sometimes still used.

Later botanists discovered that the nasturtium and the cresses belong to quite different families. They insisted on keeping the name of nasturtium for the cress plants, which had it first; and if you look it up in a botanical book today, that is where you will find it. Meanwhile, the garden nasturtium needed a scientific name, and it was given the splendid title of *Tropaeolum*, from the Greek word *tropaion*, meaning "trophy." The plant's round, shieldlike leaves and golden, helmet-shaped flowers reminded Linnaeus of the battle trophies of ancient Greece and Rome, when shields and helmets taken from the beaten foe were hung up on victory columns. However, the public persisted in calling the tropaeolums "nasturtiums," and the name stuck.

In some countries the common name of the nasturtium tells us that the shape of the flower reminded people of the pointed hoods worn by Capuchin monks. (Not the color—Capuchins wear somber brown.) In France, for instance, the name is *capucine*; in Spain, *capuchina*; in Germany, *Kapuzinerkresse* (Capuchin cress).

In Elizabethan times, not only the leaves but also the flowers of nasturtiums were used in "sallets," as salads were then called. The buds were also pickled as a relish. One species of nasturtium, grown in Peru, has a bulbous root that is eaten like a potato.

Gardeners today sometimes plant nasturtiums near their rosebushes to attract aphids. Aphids, or plant lice, are small, wingless insects that live on the juices they suck out of plants. The aphids grow strong and healthy and have thousands of offspring, but the plants grow weak and sickly and sometimes die. Since aphids prefer nasturtiums over many other plants, they serve as decoys to lure the aphids away from the plants the gardeners want to protect. Nasturtiums are also popular garden flowers in their own right.

In the nineteenth-century language of flowers, the nasturtium stands for patriotism—but it will surely never replace the flag.

Nicotiana

is named for Jean Nicot, a French diplomat who introduced tobacco to France. Nicot was born in 1530, not long after Cortez conquered Mexico, and all Europe was excited about the marvelous new animals and plants the Spanish conquerors were finding in the New World. As a young man, Nicot could have talked with men who remembered the excitement of Columbus' first voyage.

Young Nicot entered the diplomatic service of his country, and before he was thirty he was assigned to Lisbon as the French consul. This was an important position, for Portugal was then one of the world's great powers, with colonies in Brazil, Africa, India, China, and the East Indies.

Thanks to her strategically located possessions, her strong navy, and her large merchant fleet, Portugal pretty much controlled the lucrative Oriental spice trade. In West Africa, Portuguese merchants traded with the black rulers for gold and slaves. A portion of the profits from all these activities went to the king of Portugal, who became one of the world's richest sovereigns. This was the background against which Nicot operated. His mission: to keep the King and his advisers friendly to France.

In 1559 a Belgian merchant in Lisbon, with whom Nicot was friendly, gave him a present of tobacco. Something was known about tobacco already, for Columbus had described how the natives of the West Indies inhaled the smoke of the burning leaves through a forked tube they inserted in their noses. They called this inhaler *tabaco*, but the Spaniards transferred the name to the plant whose smoke they inhaled. Later adventurers had seen the Mexicans smoking, but Europeans had not yet taken up the habit, and tobacco was a mere curiosity.

Nicot presented some of his tobacco to the king and queen of Portugal, hoping to gain favor by this gift of the strange herb from the New World. The Portuguese royal pair tried it and liked it. When Nicot returned to France the next year, he took some tobacco along to give his sovereign, the notorious Catherine de Medici. She, too, was delighted with the gift, and the nobles of the court were quick to copy her. Soon smoking was all the rage in France.

A doctor named Nicholas Monardes investigated the medicinal possibilities of tobacco. From people who had been to the New World he learned that not only did the Indians smoke the dried leaves, but also chewed them to relieve hunger pangs and numb the pain of toothache.

145

Chewed tobacco leaves were used as poultices on cuts and bruises and skin diseases. Smoking the leaves was supposed to cure colds. Monardes recorded all this lore in a book in which he did his best to promote the use of tobacco as a drug. Since he was a friend of Nicot's, he mentioned Nicot prominently in the book. Not surprisingly, Nicot is known better for bringing tobacco to France than for anything else he accomplished during his long career.

The French named the tobacco plant *nicotiane* in Nicot's honor, and botanists latinized the word to *Nicotiana*, its scientific name. People began to grow tobacco in Europe, although the quality was not as good as that of American tobacco. Since the plant had attractive flowers, it was sometimes planted in gardens for ornament. In time it was observed that certain types of tobacco plants were better for flowers than for smoking, and our flowering nicotianas are descended from these, plus other species that were discovered later.

The nicotiana belongs to the nightshade family; its relatives include the petunia, potato, tomato, and eggplant. It probably originated in South America and spread into North America as the custom of smoking spread among the Indians from tribe to neighboring tribe. The leaves of the tobacco plant contain a poisonous substance, nicotine, which has a slight narcotic effect. This narcotic effect may be the reason why some people smoke much more than is good for their health and have such trouble quitting.

It is pleasant to note that Nicot survived the hazards of working for Catherine de Medici—a short-tempered and vindictive woman whose family were famous for disposing of people they disliked by poison or assassination—and died at the ripe old age of seventy.

Orchid

We usually think of orchids as exotic tropical flowers that can be grown only in greenhouses in most parts of the United States. This is true of some types, but the orchid family is very large—over 15,000 species are known, and more are always being discovered—and some species of orchid grow wild as far north as Labrador, in Canada. In fact, orchids grow in almost every part of the world except the far north, Antarctica, and desert regions.

The types of orchids raised by florists come from the tropics, and they grow on the bark of trees in rain forests. They are not parasites, for they do not harm the trees. They get all the water they need from the plentiful rainfall, and their nourishment comes from bits of decaying bark and leaves that accumulate in the tangle of their clinging roots. Plants of this type are called *epiphytes,* from the Greek *epi,* "upon," and *phyton,* "plant."

But most orchids live on the ground, and they have bulbous, fleshy roots. The ancient Greeks thought these roots resembled testicles (*orchis,* in Greek) and named the plant accordingly.

Most of the orchids sold by florists belong to two general: *Cattleya* and *Cymbidium*. The cattleyas are large, spectacular flowers, five to ten inches across. They are usually rosy-purple or white in color. They are native to Central and South America, but they are named for an Englishman, William Cattley, an ardent grower of rare plants, who died in 1832. Cattleyas were a popular, though expensive, corsage flower, the kind of flower a man would buy his wife for their wedding anniversary or, if he were not married, would use to make a big impression on his date.

The *cymbidiums* are smaller and considerably less expensive than the cattleyas, and they last much longer. Their blossoms range from three to five inches across, and they may be white, pink, yellow, brown, yellow-green, or purple. They often have an attractive spotted pattern. Most of the cymbidiums are native to southeastern Asia. The name "cymbidium" comes from *kymbe*, one of the Greek words for "boat," and refers to the shape of the flower's lip.

One of the loveliest spring wildflowers of North America is the lady-slipper, a hardy orchid that grows in cool, shady woods and at the edges of bogs. Lady-slippers were named

because they reminded early English explorers of the slippers worn by fashionable ladies in the late 1500's, when Queen Elizabeth was on the throne of England. They grow from Canada to Georgia, and west as far as the Great Plains. One species grows over most of North America. Indians of the Rocky Mountain region used to make a sleeping medicine from it. There are pink, white, and yellow lady-slippers. The pink-and-white Showy Lady-slipper is the state flower of Minnesota.

One of the orchid family is grown for its seed pods, not its flowers. This is the vanilla orchid, which is native to southern Mexico and Central America and is now raised in many tropical countries. The Aztecs used vanilla pods to flavor their dark, bitter chocolate drink, and the Spaniards took the custom back to Europe. Vanilla pods look like large, dark-brown string beans; the Spaniards thought they looked like the sheath of a knife or sword and named them *vainilla*, from *vaina*, meaning "sheath," plus the ending *-illa*, which carries the meaning of "little." In English this became "vanilla."

From a spice for hot chocolate, vanilla grew to be one of the world's most popular flavorings. It was often sold in the form of vanilla extract, a liquid about as alcoholic as whiskey or gin. Sometimes people who liked a nip but thought liquor was sinful—or who didn't want neighbors to smell it on their breath—drank vanilla extract. Nowadays much of the world's vanilla flavoring is made cheaply from byproducts of paper manufacturing. The genuine article is used only in higher-priced foods. But if you remember that the tiny specks of real vanilla bean in your ice cream are really the seeds of exotic tropical orchids, the price may not seem so bad.

Pansy

The pansy is a large, showy cousin of the modest violet. It is descended from a wild European violet that used to be considered a weed of grain fields and gardens. Although this wild pansy, *Viola tricolor* (Latin for "three-colored violet"), was known to Europeans for centuries, the pansy as we know it today did not exist before the 1800's.

The story is that around 1812 an English noblewoman had her gardener plant some wild pansies in a heart-shaped bed in her wildflower garden. In this romantic setting they crossed naturally with other species of wild violet. The result was a hybrid with much bigger flowers and a much greater variety of colors than its wild ancestors. About the same time, a nearby lord had a similar wild garden planted on his estate, and his gardener bred many improved strains of pansies from the natural crosses. He bred so many, in fact, that he ran out of names for them and had to use the names of characters in Shakespeare's plays. (Shakespeare himself actually mentioned the pansy only once by that name; in *Hamlet* he had Ophelia say, ". . . there's pansies, that's for thoughts.")

The name "pansy" is of French origin. It comes from *pensée*, the French word for "thought," and it entered the English language around 1500. Englishmen (and women, too) soon changed the French "pawn-say" to the English "pansy." Why the flower became an emblem of thought is hard to say—perhaps because with some imagination you can see a pensive human face in the markings of the blossoms.

In the language of flowers a bunch of pansies could mean "Think of me," or "I have tender and pleasant thoughts about you." This romantic association is very old. Long before Shakespeare's time, English country folk called the wild pansy by such names as "Love-in-Idleness," "Heart's Ease," and "Cull-me-neere" (that is, "Hug-me-tight"). Another name, suggested by the facelike markings, was "Three Faces in a Hood."

Pansies were apparently used to make love potions—at least Shakespeare hints at this. In the play *A Midsummer*

Night's Dream, Oberon, king of the fairies, uses pansy juice dropped on the eyes of his sleeping wife, Titania, to make her fall in love with the first creature she sees on waking. Oberon, who is having a nasty spat with Titania, arranges for that creature to be an uneducated workman who has magically been given a donkey's head. After Titania, compelled by the passionate power of the pansies, has made herself thoroughly ridiculous, Oberon relents and lifts the spell. Shakespeare would probably not have used the pansy in this plot unless there was already a common belief in its amorous powers.

Pansies were used in medicine in the same ways as other violets were. In the 1500's and 1600's they found a new use in attempts to cure syphilis. The logic behind this was probably that the pansy, a flower that was supposed to arouse sexual passions, must be good for disease brought on by indulging those passions. It did not work.

"Pansy" was once a popular girls' name. By an unreasoning association of flowers with women, it also came to mean an effeminate man or boy. (Males striving to be accepted as rough, tough he-men were duty-bound to consider flowers "unmanly.") This was unfair to all parties concerned, including the flower.

Peony

To peoples of the ancient world many plants were magical, and one of the most magical was the peony. The Greeks believed that peonies shone at night when the moon was full (in fact, the reflection of moonlight off the shiny leaves can produce this effect) and that they had the power to drive away demons. The roots of the peony could work miraculous cures. But the gods were jealous of such powerful magic, and they set giant woodpeckers to guard the wild peonies of Greece. The plants had to be gathered by night, for by day the woodpeckers would peck out the eyes of any impious mortal who ventured near. But extra precautions were necessary. Even at night it was dangerous to dig up peonies, for as the plant was pulled from the ground, it gave a groan of such supernatural anguish that it killed anyone who heard it. Therefore, a peony hunter had to tie a dog to the plant with a very strong cord, stuff his ears, stand back, and lure the dog toward him with a piece of roasted meat. When the dog lunged for the meat, he pulled up the peony, perishing as he carried out his master's command. At least this was the story the herb gatherers told, and the philosophers believed.

Of course, such a miraculous plant had to have a miraculous origin, and the Greeks supplied a fitting legend. When the Trojan War was being fought, some of the gods fought along on each side. The god Pluto, fighting for the Trojans, was severely wounded by Hercules. In the Trojan camp was a man named Paeon, who was physician to the gods. (In other versions of the legend, Paeon is one of the titles of Apollo.) Now, Paeon owned a piece of magical peony root, and with this he instantly healed Pluto's wound. Unfortunately word of this miracle cure reached Aesculapius, the god of healing, and he worked himself into such a passion of jealousy that he vowed to kill Paeon. But the grateful Pluto saved Paeon from death by turning him into the flower with which he had healed the god, and which now bears his name.

Greeks and Romans used the peony to cure many ailments, but above all to treat epilepsy and nightmares. These diseases, they believed, were caused by unusually powerful and malicious demons, and the strong countermagic of peonies was needed to drive them away. If the cure did not work, a clever physician could always blame its failure on the displeasure of the gods.

The ancient superstitious lore about the peony was passed on from generation to generation, growing as each generation added its own nuggets of misinformation, until by the end of the Middle Ages it got to be too much for intelligent people to believe. But physicians still had faith in the peony's curative powers, and even as late as the 1600's they prescribed it. And down to the end of the 1800's, peony roots were made into strings of beads for babies to teethe on.

Roman colonists may have brought peonies to Britain. At any rate, by the 1300's Englishmen were quite familiar with them. The seeds were used in cooking as a cheap substitute for pepper, and also to spice ale in peasants' taverns.

The roots were eaten as a costly delicacy at banquets of kings and the richest nobles. Since peony roots are tough even after hours of cooking, they were usually minced to reduce the amount of chewing that had to be done. They could not have been too tasty, either, since one recipe called for them to be served with a sauce of onions, salt, and garlic, which would drown almost any taste. However, they were expensive, and that was what counted most when it came to making impressions.

Peonies also went into a very complicated medieval dessert made with peony root, raisins, sandalwood, pepper, cinnamon, ale, wine, vinegar, almonds, honey, ginger, saffron, and salt. This was cooked and cooked until it was good and thick, then served "alle flat on a dysshe, alle hote." It was not popular for very long.

The old recipe books spelled "peony" as "pioun," "pyoun," "peiounie," "pyiony," and many other ways. In Anglo-Saxon times it was spelled "peone." Eighteenth-century botanists, displaying their classical learning, used the spelling "paeony," and the peony's modern botanical name uses the old Greek form, *paeonia*.

The peony belongs to the buttercup family, and it is native to many parts of the northern hemisphere, including the western United States. It is Indiana's state flower. The finest kinds, however, come from China and Japan, where they have been cultivated for thousands of years. They were first introduced to the West in the early 1800's. Some of the Chinese peonies have flowers so big that the plants must be staked up to support them. From China, too, come the tree peonies (actually bushes), which grow as tall as six feet and bear up to 300 flowers at one time. It is said that tree peonies can live as long as 200 years.

Peony flowers are usually red, pink, or white; there are also yellow varieties. In one of the floral languages, the deep-red peony signifies "bashful shame." (The flower is supposedly blushing over its bad smell.) Peonies can also carry the meaning of ostentation ("You're a big show-off"), anger, indignation, confidential message, and timidity ("I'm too shy to tell you in words, but . . ."). It takes a magical flower indeed to express so many meanings, and such contradictory ones.

Petunia

In the early 1820's a French scientific expedition discovered a new wildflower in southern Brazil. The flower, which was white and bloomed at night, had a wonderfully sweet scent. It looked like the flower of the tobacco plant, but the scientists couldn't quite place it, and they sent it back to Paris to be classified. A leading botanist there named it *petunia*, from *petun* (an old French name for "tobacco"), which comes from a South American Indian name for tobacco, *pety*. The name was a good choice, for the petunia is closely related to the tobacco plant. Both belong to the nightshade family.

Seeds of the white petunia were sent to Europe from South America, and in 1831 a Scottish merchant in Argentina sent home seeds of a wild purple petunia that flowered by day. Our modern garden petunias are descended from crosses between these two wild species. Today you can grow petunias in a wide range of reds, pinks, and blues, as well as purple and white. Interestingly, petunias that are left to seed themselves tend to produce small scrubby plants with flowers of an unattractive purple shade, probably like their wild ancestors.

Petunias are hard to grow from seed, but once they are started they grow with little care. Gardeners like them because they grow in almost any kind of soil and produce masses of flowers. They are popular for gardens, pots, and windowboxes. Hummingbirds are fond of petunias (they feed on the nectar), which is one of the nicest reasons for growing them.

In one of the old dictionaries of flower language, the petunia meant "Thou art less proud than they deem thee." This message might have been sent by a young man to a hard-to-please girl with whom he had made a hit—if it were ever actually sent at all.

Poinsettia

is named for Joel Poinsett, a nineteenth-century politician and diplomat. Poinsett was born in Charleston, South Carolina, in 1779. As a boy he wanted more than anything else to become a soldier, but his father, a doctor, dissuaded him. Instead, Poinsett traveled widely, aided the various South American movements to win independence

159

from Spain, and in between adventures took part in politics in his home state. He served in Congress from 1821 to 1825, then was named as the first United States ambassador to the new republic of Mexico. Unfortunately Poinsett took too active an interest in the politics of Mexico. He was implicated in a quarrel between factions of Mexican politicians and accused of helping one faction to plot an armed takeover of the government. The faction he was friendly with lost the struggle for power, and in 1830 Poinsett was ordered out of the country by the winning clique.

While in Mexico, Poinsett was attracted by a common wild shrub that blossomed with rosettes of brilliant red petals in the winter. (Botanists will tell you that the red petals of the poinsettia are actually colored bracts, or specialized leaves; the true flowers are the little yellow things in the middle of the red rosettes.) He brought specimens back to the United States with him and developed ornamental varieties with bigger "flowers." The poinsettia became popular as a house plant because it could be made to flower in the dead of winter, when almost nothing else could. Nurserymen popularized it as a Christmas decoration. In Sweden its name is *julstjärna*, "Christmas Star."

The poinsettia belongs to the spurge family, so called because their milky, irritating sap was used in ancient times for the same purpose as castor oil is used today. (*Spurge* comes from *purge*, which means to clean or purify or get rid of impurities.) Some of its relatives are the rubber tree, the castor-oil plant, and the manioc plant, from which tapioca is made. However, the poinsettia yields neither food, rubber, nor laxative. Its only use is to delight the eye.

160

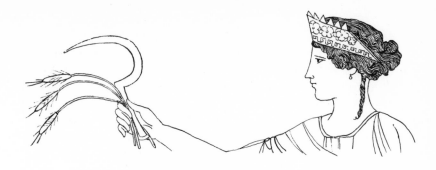

Poppy

Since time immemorial men have known of the narcotic qualities of the milky-white juice of the poppy. An ancient Egyptian papyrus scroll written 3,500 years ago contains a recipe for a sleeping medicine for crying children made with poppies. The Greeks, too, knew of the poppy's sleep-inducing power, and they explained this in one of their many myths.

Demeter, the goddess of all growing things, went into a terrible depression when her daughter Persephone was kidnapped by Pluto, the god of the underworld, to be his wife. She could not sleep for grief, and she refused to make the crops grow. Without their crops, mankind would starve, and without men and women to worship them, the gods would be in a bad way. Therefore, the god of sleep created the poppy to put Demeter to sleep. She awoke much refreshed, and the crops revived. For this reason—or perhaps because poppies often grow wild in grain fields—the Greeks usually portrayed Demeter wearing a garland of ears of grain with poppies woven into it.

The Greeks called the poppy *mekon*, but our name for it comes from the Latin name, *papaver*. In late Roman times this became *papavum*. German tribes along Rome's north-western frontier picked up the word and turned it into *popag*. The Anglo-Saxons, who came originally from north-west Germany, called it *popaeg*. By the Middle Ages, this had softened into *popi*, and the modern form dates from about the 1500's.

But poppies grew wild all over Europe, and they had many native names. The native German name, for instance, is *Mohn*; in Spanish the poppy is called *amapola*; in Swedish, *vallmo*, which originally may have meant "pasture-flower"; in French, *coquelicot*, which is almost the same thing French roosters say when they crow.

Poppies belong to the poppy family, and they are native to Europe, North Africa, and Asia. A few species of poppy are native to the western United States. The golden poppy, a cousin of the true poppy, is the state flower of California.

The oldest cultivated poppy is the opium poppy, which probably originated in the eastern Mediterranean area. Its scientific name is *Papaver somniferum* (Latin for "sleep-bringing poppy"). Opium is a gummy, dark-colored substance made from the dried juice of the seed pods of the opium poppy. It was probably named in the first century A.D. by the Greek medical writer Dioscorides, who called it *opion*, from *opos*, the Greek term for vegetable juice. In Latin this became *opium*.

The Greeks and Romans knew the value of opium for relieving pain and sleeplessness. They also knew that too large a dose of opium could cause death. During the Middle Ages opium was not much used, perhaps because the Church taught that it was sinful for men to escape the pains that according to the Church were sent by God. However, there was a sleeping medicine, which the English called "dwale," that contained opium along with henbane, lettuce, bryony (a vine related to the cucumber), and hemlock, all boiled together in the gall of a boar. Two of the plants in the recipe, hemlock and henbane, contain powerful narcotic poisons; so dwale must have been risky to use. A medical manuscript from the 1300's tells how dwale can be used to put a patient to sleep for an operation, but that is the only record of its use in medicine.

163

In the 1500's things changed. Many quack remedies containing opium were invented, and marvelous curative powers were claimed for them. Of course, they could not cure any disease, but the opium did relieve discomfort and pain for a few hours. One of the most famous of these quack remedies was called laudanum. Invented by a sixteenth-century medical rebel named Paracelsus, who also made some real contributions to medicine, laudanum originally contained gold, pearls, coral, powdered mummies, amber, musk, and other costly ingredients. It was obviously a luxury drug, intended for the very rich. However, around 1800 someone invented a stripped-down version of laudanum, containing only opium and alcohol, which could be made and sold very cheaply. Working-class mothers in England often used laudanum to quiet their hungry children—it was cheaper than food—and drank it themselves instead of tea or gin. For a little while it made them forget the misery of their lives.

But the half-starved wives of underpaid factory hands were not the only ones who took to opium. A cult of opium eating grew up in England's literary and artistic circles. These more or less gifted souls believed that the lovely visions produced by the opium trance would inspire them to create truly great works of art. This was very seldom the case, although one poet, Samuel Taylor Coleridge, produced some of his finest work while under the influence of opium. A writer named Thomas de Quincey achieved fame and a good deal of money by writing about his own opium addiction. But most of the would-be artists simply became addicts. Lacking talent to begin with, they could not acquire it from a drug.

Thanks to the poor—not so much to the artists, for there weren't nearly as many of them—there was such demand for opium in the early 1800's that it was actually raised in England. One opium farmer calculated that a single acre of poppies would yield fifty-six pounds of opium, while the seeds, as a bonus, would yield 375 pints of the finest salad oil.

Opium was probably taken to China by Arab traders in the thirteenth century A.D. For a long time it was used only as a medicine. Then in the 1600's the Chinese learned how to smoke opium for "highs", and addiction became a problem. Repressive laws did nothing to stop the abuse of opium. At the end of the 1700's the government of China forbade the importation of "foreign mud," as the Chinese called the drug. However, as has happened in other countries trying to control other drugs, smugglers, aided by corrupt officials, managed to keep China's addicts supplied with all the opium they could smoke.

Most of China's opium came from India, which was then controlled by Britain, although it had not yet been declared a part of the British Empire. In 1839 Chinese warships opened fire on British opium ships from India, and Britain had an excuse for declaring war. The war went into the history books as the Opium War. Its real object was to force China to let British goods in for sale, but a more sordid excuse could hardly have been found.

From opium are prepared the more potent and dangerous drugs morphine and heroin. Abuse of these drugs has become such a threat to public health that almost every country in the world has banned them. In many countries it is also forbidden to raise opium poppies.

But opium was not the only medicinal use of the poppy. The Egyptians used poppies in laxatives and foot medicines. The Assyrians used it for many things; they also used the root of the poppy as an aphrodisiac. The Greeks, too, used poppies in a very strong laxative, while half way around the world, Indian tribes used poppies to treat colds, gout, headache, and pleurisy. The juice was used as a sleeping medicine, to stop the pain of a toothache, and to remove warts.

The Romans used poppy seeds to flavor bread and started a fashion that is still with us. The little black seeds on seeded rolls are poppy seeds (they do not contain opium), and poppy seeds are used in a number of pastries. Long before Rome was mighty, Greek athletes trained for the Olympic Games on poppy seed mixed with wine and honey. The oil from poppy seeds is used in some countries for cooking and salad oil. It is also used in artists' paints.

Some of the most popular species of garden poppies are the Iceland poppy (which really comes from Siberia), the

quets. It was not uncommon for a host to have the dining couches covered with rose petals for the guests to recline on, while the tables and floors might also be strewn with rose petals. For a really impressive splurge, the host might have the street outside his mansion covered with rose petals. Inside the house, garlands of roses festooned the walls, and the rose was the most popular flower for the wreaths the revelers wore on their heads or around their necks. To supply the thousands of roses these customs required, enterprising men in the Roman colonies began growing them on a huge scale for export to the mother country. Egypt was one of the biggest rose growers, although it is not known how the flowers were kept fresh during the long trip to Rome. Perhaps whole bushes were dug up and shipped in pots.

Because of the close links between the rose and the scandalous pagan orgies of Rome, the early Christian church looked on the flower with horror and loathing. Yet a few centuries later it had become one of the emblems of the Virgin Mary and a symbol of purity. The beads used by Roman Catholics to keep count of their prayers are called a "rosary," a word which originally meant a rose garden, but which romantic monks of the Middle Ages used for a series h⟨f⟩ repeated prayers, which they compared to the flowers in co⟨r⟩ Virgin Mary's rose garden. Eventually the name was gion⟨ied⟩ to the beads as well as to the prayers.

iest b⟨s⟩es were one of the staples of ancient medicine. A few these ⟨⟩ ailments for which they were used were headache, After ⟨t⟩al troubles, wounds, skin diseases, tumors, and ra- formed ⟨t⟩es continued in medical use down into the 1700's, poppies to ⟨⟩water, prepared by distilling rose petals, was a I are alive no⟨⟩nt of perfumes and cosmetics.

⟨r⟩ose perfumes are prepared not with rose

water, but with the pure essential oil, or attar, of roses. While attar of roses is made in a number of places in Europe and the Middle East, the finest attar comes from Bulgaria.

Before modern methods came into use, squads of rose pickers would go out in the early summer mornings, before the sun had dried the dew from the petals, and pick sacks full of the flowers while they were at the height of their fragrance. The petals were then put into huge pottery jars, and water was added to fill the jars to the top. After many hours the fragrant oil from the petals would float to the surface, where it could be skimmed off. Today the attar is distilled by steam, but it still takes about ten *tons* of rose petals to make one *pound* of attar; so the price is understandably high. As a result, attar of roses is often adulterated with geranium oil or synthetic rose essence.

Roses belong to the rose family, one of the largest and most important families of cultivated plants. Many of our most familiar fruits belong to the rose family: apples, pears, peaches, plums, cherries, apricots, raspberries, blackberries, and strawberries. The fruits of the rose itself, called "hips," are eaten in some countries. While some roses have hips about the size of a pencil eraser and just about as tasty, other kinds bear fruits that look like a small tomato and taste like a pleasantly tart, soft apple. These hips are rich in vitamin C, and they can be made into jelly. In the Scandinavian countries they are also made into a kind of thick soup, which is topped off with sweetened whipped cream.

Rose petals were formerly candied, and rose water used to be a standard flavoring in the kitchens of those who could afford it. Centuries earlier, the Romans made a bizarre but satisfyingly costly banquet dish from stewed calves' brains and rose petals.

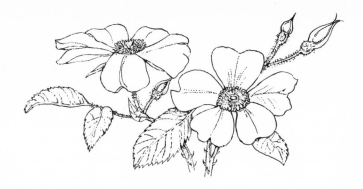

Roses grow wild in many regions of the northern hemisphere. The wild roses are usually "single" flowers, that is, their blossoms have just one set of petals. This makes for a rather flat flower. Cultivated roses, however, are usually "double," that is, they have two or more sets of petals, which produce a bigger, fuller flower.

Through centuries of cultivation men have bred thousands of varieties of roses. Some have been bred mainly for their scent, others for appearance. One kind of rose has such big flowers that they have been compared to cabbages. It is called, not surprisingly, the cabbage rose. There are roses that bloom early in the season and roses that bloom late, and some varieties bloom most of the summer, except in the very hottest part. There are pigmy roses the size of a quarter that grow on bushes six inches high, and there are roses nearly as big as a tennis ball, on very large and thorny bushes. There are also the old-fashioned climbing roses, whose long, limber branches look almost like vines. Wild roses are usually pink or white, but cultivated roses come in just about every imaginable shade of red, pink, orange, yellow, white, and even lavender. And today the rose is the emblem of four American states: Georgia, Iowa, New York, and North Dakota.

The name "rose" has been given to some flowers that are not related to the rose at all. One is the rose of Sharon, which belongs to the mallow family and is related to the hollyhock and the hibiscus. Another is the primrose, which belongs to the buttercup family; the Christmas rose, or hellebore, also belongs to the buttercup family. The rose of Jericho belongs to the mustard family. In the Scandinavian countries the sunflower is called "sun rose."

One "rose" that is not a flower at all is the compass rose, a design sometimes drawn on maps to indicate all the points of the compass. Centuries ago, mapmakers decorated this functional design to look like a flower, hence the name.

In the language of flowers roses could mean anything from "the heart that knows not love" to "I am worthy of you," depending on the color and variety of the rose. But almost every meaning was connected with love. Although the flower language has long since gone the way of the horse and buggy, a bouquet of roses still carries the message "I love you," as it did in the days when the Greeks were worshipping Aphrodite.

In England in the late 1400's there was a long period of civil warfare known as the Wars of the Roses. The king was weak, foolish, and too incompetent to defend his own interests, and two powerful noble families were battling for control of the king and succession to the throne. One of the rival families was the great House of York, the other, the House of Lancaster. The story goes that before their quarrel had reached the point of open war, and while they were still jockeying for support from the other nobles, some of the leading men of both sides were strolling in the king's rose garden. An argument broke out, and the leader of the Yorkist faction picked a white rose, saying, "Everyone who is with me, wear this for your badge." The chief of the Lancaster party then picked a red rose for his badge, and the conflict had its name.

Most of the fighting was done by professional soldiers, who shifted freely back and forth between York and Lancaster according to who paid better. Many of the noblemen, driven by greed or by grudges, shifted their allegiance likewise. Some historians say that each faction was cordially detested in its home territory, and both sides ended up being hated throughout England because of the brutality and greed of their soldiers. The Lancastrians gained an early advantage when they got control of the king, but they lost most of the battles. Eventually the Yorkists won, but they tactfully adopted a red *and* a white rose as an emblem of unity. In his tragedy, Romeo and Juliet, Shakespeare had Juliet sigh, "a rose by any other name would smell as sweet." This is true, of course, but poets can be thankful that the rose is not called paphiopedilum or machaeranthera.

Snapdragon

is named for the shape of the flower—a little like the snout
of the stylized dragon painted on medieval coats of arms—
and for the fact that by squeezing it at its base you can
make it open up like a mouth; when you release the
pressure, the open "jaws" snap shut. An old name for
the flower was "Lion's Mouth"—apparently some people
must have thought the flower looked more like a lion than a
dragon. In a number of countries it is called "lion's mouth"
or something very close: In Italy, for example, it is called
bocca di leone ("mouth of lion"); in Germany, *Löwenmaul*
("lion's mouth"); in Sweden, *lejongap* ("lion's gaping
mouth"). The Spaniards, however, agree with the English;
they call it *boca de dragón* ("mouth of dragon").

Another old name for the snapdragon was "Calves' Snout," from the fancied resemblance between its seed pods and the muzzle of a calf. The French took this viewpoint, for their name for the snapdragon, *muflier*, means, roughly, "snouter." (It comes from *mufle*, the French word for an animal's snout or muzzle.) The scientific name of the snapdragon, *Antirrhinum*, is Greek for "snoutlike," from *anti-*, which in Greek means "like," plus *rhis, rhino-*, "nose."

The snapdragon, a native of southern Europe, belongs to the family of *Scrophularaceae*, so named because one member of the family, the figwort, was formerly used in a remedy for the skin disease called scrofula. Another familiar member of the family is the foxglove.

Snapdragon was also the name of an English Christmas game of a rather messy sort. The players tried to snatch raisins out of a bowl of flaming brandy and eat them while they were still burning. The one who swallowed the most flaming raisins was the winner. This must have been one game in which the losers came out ahead.

Sweet Pea

is a cousin of the garden pea. It is named for its sweet odor, not for its flavor. In fact, its pealike seeds are poisonous. The name *pea* itself comes from the Latin word for a pea, *pisum*. In Anglo-Saxon this became *pise* (pronounced pea-zuh), which later came to be written as *pease*. A pease meant just one pea; more than one were pease*n*. But gradually English-speakers lost the old habit of making plurals by adding *-n* and began to use *-s* instead. So, in time, people came to think that *pease* was plural and that the singular form must be *pea*. So ever since the late 1600's we have said pea and peas instead of pease and peasen.

The sweet pea is a native of Sicily, where it grew wild and attracted no attention until a science-minded priest, Father

Franciscus Cupani, described it in a botanical handbook in 1697. For more than a century after that sweet peas were raised only on a small scale, as floral curiosities. Not until the 1870's did they start to gain popularity. It was in the reign of Queen Victoria's playboy son, King Edward VII, some thirty years later, that the sweet pea truly came into its own.

As it happened, the sweet pea was the favorite flower of Edward's royal spouse, Alexandra; and when Edward finally reached the throne after waiting on the sidelines for fifty-nine years, the new Queen's preference was enough to launch the sweet pea on its way to success. The sweet pea was the "in" flower for Edwardians. Men wore it in their buttonholes; women filled their flower vases with it; it bloomed from centerpieces on fashionable dinner tables; it was a must for weddings. The sweet-pea craze ran its course and disappeared long ago, but the flower is still popular.

The imaginative compilers of floral languages disagreed on many points, but they all seemed to agree that the sweet pea signified departure. Was this because they knew it was poisonous?

Tulip

Men have gambled with cards and dice; they have, more respectably, gambled on the stock market; they have wagered huge sums on horse races. But one of the strangest gambling manias in history involved the tulip.

First we must go back a bit in time. Tulips grow wild from the Mediterranean region eastward across Asia to Japan. But the first people that are known to have raised them as garden flowers were the Turks. We do not know just when or where the Turks began raising the colorful wildflower, but it was certainly before 1500. The Turks, good Moslems that they were, noticed that a tulip flower turned upside down looked rather like a turban, the headgear that Moslem men were commanded to wear as an emblem of their faith. They called the flower *tulband* or *tulliband*, both Turkish mispronunciations of the original Persian word for "turban," *dulband*.

In the mid-1550's a Belgian-born diplomat named Ogier de Busbecq arrived in Constantinople, capital of the Turkish empire. He represented the Austrian empire, and his mission was to negotiate peace with the Turks, who had overrun North Africa and large areas of southern and central Europe. While there, de Busbecq was most impressed by the Turkish gardens filled with red and yellow "tullibands" (these were the colors the Turks preferred), and he sent seeds and bulbs back to the imperial court at Vienna. From there, tulips spread to nearby parts of Europe.

At this point another Belgian-born character enters the plot, the famous botanist Clusius. Clusius, who could speak eight languages, supervised the imperial gardens at Vienna for many years. About 1590 he was appointed professor of botany at the new University of Leyden, in the Netherlands, and he took a choice collection of tulip bulbs with him. At Leyden he planted a splendid tulip garden and rejoiced in the admiration of visitors. Many of the visitors asked to buy a bulb or two, but Clusius demanded such high prices that no one could afford to pay them. Perhaps Clusius asked unreasonable prices on purpose, in order to keep the tulips for himself, but if this was the case he was sadly and badly disappointed. Covetous flower lovers stole his best tulips from his garden by night, and soon tulip bulbs and seeds were being sold openly all over Europe.

In the various countries of Europe, people twisted the Turkish name of *tulliband* into forms they found more comfortable, such as *tulipan, tulipe, Tulpe, tulp,* and *tulip.* But rich men still sent direct to Turkey for the finest tulip bulbs. Meanwhile, the Dutch were beginning to take the lead in Europe in tulip growing. They had an almost unlimited market, for the passion for growing tulips spread from the rich to the middle classes, and no one with any claim to culture would be caught without a bed of tulips in his garden.

The demand for tulips led people to buy and sell bulbs on speculation, in the hope of making a huge profit. It often happened that the bulb itself did not change hands, while people bought the rights to it and sold them again for double the price. By the 1630's, even the poorest people in the Netherlands had been hit by the tulip mania, and the middle classes were selling their houses, land, and possessions at ridiculously low prices in order to raise more money to buy tulips. It seemed as if the boom would never end. Englishmen, Frenchmen, and other eager foreigners bought all the bulbs the Dutch could supply. And the bulbs sold for fantastic prices. A single bulb of *Semper Augustus*, a particularly prized variety, sold for the equivalent of five thousand dollars in cash, plus a new carriage, two handsome gray horses, and a complete set of harness, which must have been worth as much again.

Some horrible misadventures occurred during the height of the tulip mania. There is one story of a rich merchant who left a valuable bulb, worth about $2,500, on the counter of his office when he went home for lunch. His servant, who was minding the office in his absence, thought that the bulb was an onion and would go very well with his own lunch of a red herring. When the merchant returned, the bulb was missing and the servant was picking his teeth.

The merchant's reaction is not recorded.

Another story tells of an English traveler who fancied himself an expert botanist. While visiting a Dutch acquaintance he, too, saw a tulip bulb lying about. Not knowing what it was, he took out his penknife and began to dissect the bulb layer by layer, all the time uttering expert-sounding remarks on the unusual onion. At length he grew tired of this experiment and cut the remainder of the bulb in half, calling his host to come and look at this most extraordinary specimen. The outraged Dutchman hauled him off to court, and he stayed in jail until he had repaid the price of the ruined tulip.

The truth of these stories cannot be guaranteed, but stock markets just for tulips were actually set up in the main cities of the Netherlands, and specialists in bulb trading did their best to drive the price continually up. However, the bubble finally burst. The natural caution of the Dutch reasserted itself. The more sensible people realized that the boom could not go on forever. One by one, they stopped buying. Prices fell. It was like the collapse of a chain-letter scheme. People who had contracted to buy tulips at, say, $1,000 refused to honor their pledges when the price of the bulbs at delivery time had dropped to $100. Panic set in, and by the end of 1636 the government had to step in to keep the country from complete ruin. Tulip dealers in London and Paris had also tried to play the same game of speculation, but without such notable success as the Dutch. Therefore, less damage was done in England and France when the tulip boom collapsed.

In spite of the disaster, bulbs of rare varieties continued to fetch a fancy price, and in the mid-1800's one Englishman complained that a single tulip bulb would bring more money than an oak tree or twelve acres of wheat.

The tulip is a member of the lily family, and its relatives include lily of the valley, asparagus, and onion. Tulip bulbs are edible, and in the 1600's some people ate them like onions (just as in the story). One Englishman wrote in his diary, "boyled and buttered, they make a rare dish." Another liked them preserved and candied in sugar syrup. Sir Kenelm Digby, an English politician who also invented a number of quack remedies, recommended the tulip's seed pods. When boiled, he said, they tasted like peas. After the 1600's tulips were not eaten for a very long time. Then, in World War II, the Germans occupied the Netherlands and seized most of the food. The starving Dutch people, in desperation, ate tulip bulbs to keep alive.

Tulips had little use in old-time medicine and, since they have no scent, they were not used in perfume or cosmetics. They were raised for their beauty alone. In the language of flowers tulips could mean "I love you" or "You have beautiful eyes." A bouquet of yellow tulips meant "I love you hopelessly." If the sender were lucky, he might get back a bouquet of Chinese sacred lilies, meaning "you may hope."

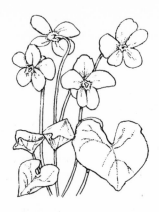

Violet

is a diminutive form of the Old French word *viole*, which comes from the Latin name for the violet, *viola*. Because of the diminutive ending *-et*, it literally means "little violet." The name came into English with the Norman Conquest.

Viola is also the Italian name for a whole family of musical instruments, including the violin ("little viola," from the Italian *violino*); the viola itself, an alto violin; the *violoncello* ("little big viola"), now usually called the cello; and the *violone* ("big viola"), an old name for the bass viol. It would be nice to think that the shape of the violas was copied from that of the flower, but apparently there is no connection between the names.

The Greek name for the violet was *ion*, and the name for the color we call violet—a bluish-purple shade—was *iodes*. In 1812 a French chemist named Courtois was boiling seaweed ashes in acid when he noticed that the mixture was giving off a bluish-purple vapor that condensed into shiny, grayish-black crystals. Suspecting that the new substance was an unknown chemical element, Courtois christened his discovery *iode*, for the violet color of its vapor. In English this became *iodine*.

No one really knows where the word *ion* came from. There have been ingenious attempts to link it with the myth of Io, a Greek princess with whom the never-wearying Zeus fell in love and had an affair. Io was a priestess of Hera, and so Hera felt doubly aggrieved at Zeus' adultery with her. But when she accused Zeus of his misdoings, he deceitfully replied that he had never touched Io. What was more, he would turn her into a cow to prove how little she meant to him. For once he was as good as his word, and poor Io found herself transformed into a white heifer and immediately claimed by Hera as compensation for her suffering. In one version of the myth, Zeus, feeling a little bit sorry for his ex-love, caused violets to spring from the ground for her to eat. This, however, was probably a late attempt to link the myth of Io with the very old word *ion*. The story of Io goes on, with horrible deeds of murder and treachery, but there is not room to tell it here.

The violet belongs to the violet family, and there are about 300 species of violets. Most are native to Europe, Asia, and North America. It is the state flower of Illinois, New Jersey, Wisconsin, and—unofficially—of Rhode Island.

The pansy is a violet created by crossing different species of wild violets and selectively breeding their descendants. Its main ancestor is *Viola tricolor*, the "three-colored violet."

A close relative is the Johnny-jump-up, so named because it grows and blooms so quickly in the spring. The African violet, however, is not a violet, but belongs to a different family.

For centuries poets have been impressed with the sweet scent of violets (although some species are odorless) and their short period of bloom, which led to many sentimental expressions of pity for the short-lived flower. Actually the short life of the violet is a superb example of evolutionary adaptation. Most violets are woodland flowers, and a woodland flower must bloom, be pollinated, and ripen its seed before the trees put out their leaves and cut off its supply of light and energy. If the flowers went on blooming in the shade, they would be wasting energy that should be going to producing seeds for the next generation of violets.

The sweet violet, named for its scent, was a favorite of the Greeks, who boasted that they could make it bloom all year round by tricks of cultivation. Violets were also used in medicine by the Greeks and Romans, and they were still being used by Europeans well into the 1600's. The Puritan settlers of New England used them, too. Violets were used in sleeping medicines and soothing syrups for pleurisy, sore throat, and coughs. Violet syrup was considered particularly good for children, but for some reason the experts recommended mixing it with "oil of vitriol," or concentrated sulfuric acid, a very dangerous chemical. A gentler remedy was made from the dried petals, which were powdered and drunk in water. In the early 1800's an American medical book was still recommending violets for colds, constipation, and kidney stones.

Violets were also used for food. Candied violets have been eaten as a treat since medieval times, and one experimental Englishman of the seventeenth century recommended fried violet leaves flavored with orange or lemon juice and sugar. In Europe a liqueur is made with violets. A beautiful light purple in color, it smells like perfume.

One of the major uses of violets today is in the perfume industry, but most of the violet perfume comes from the root of a kind of iris. The perfume is chemically identical, but the iris contains more of it and is easier to harvest than millions of tiny flower blossoms.

The violet has always been a symbol of modesty and shyness, as in the old expression, "a shrinking violet," meaning someone who shrank from being noticed. Eventually this phrase was given a sarcastic twist into "shrieking violet," or someone who would do anything to get attention.

Wisteria

should really be spelled "wistaria," for its name honors a Pennsylvania doctor named Caspar Wistar. Born in Philadelphia in 1761, Wistar became a distinguished physician and medical educator. He taught chemistry at the College of Philadelphia's medical school and later taught anatomy and obstetrics at the newly created University of Pennsylvania. At the same time he served on the staff of a hospital and cared for his private patients. Somehow he found time to write the first American textbook on anatomy and to join the illustrious American Philosophical Society. This society was the first scientific society in the United States. It was founded in 1740 by Benjamin Franklin, and Thomas Jefferson was also a member. The advancement of science was a lifelong interest of Wistar's, and one night a week he held open house for scientists at his big, comfortable mansion on Fourth Street in Philadelphia.

One of the scientists he befriended was an English botanist named Nuttall, whose eccentric personality kept him permanently and desperately poor. Despite his many eccentricities, Nuttall was always made to feel welcome at Wistar's house. After Wistar died in 1818, Nuttall in gratitude named a new plant for him. (Nuttall spelled it "wisteria"—perhaps he thought it sounded better that way.)

The plant was a woody, climbing vine that had recently been introduced from China—the United States was then in the midst of a wave of enthusiasm for Chinese pottery, cloth, and flowers. The vine, which belongs to the pea family, became very popular for shading arbors and porches and for training up the sides of buildings, as it is today. Unfortunately the wisteria flowers for only a week or two in late spring or early summer, but it makes up for that by bearing such masses of flowers that it seems to be raining blossoms. In fact, in some countries it is known as "blue rain."

There are white, purple, and pink wisterias in addition to blue. Although two species of wisteria are native to the southeastern states, the first cultivated varieties came from China and Japan, and our main garden varieties are descended from these. Some of the Oriental varieties have flower clusters three to four feet long. For a show like that, one can almost forgive the plant for blooming such a short time.

Zinnia

Like its cousin the dahlia, the zinnia is a native of Mexico, where the Aztecs raised it in their gardens. The wild zinnia has rather dull purplish flowers, but the Aztec gardeners developed varieties with more color. One of the Aztec names for the zinnia was *mal-aca-xochitl*, or "spindle-flower."

Surprisingly—or perhaps not so surprisingly because the zinnia had no use in cooking or medicine—it was not brought to Europe until the 1700's. From Europe it came to the United States, in bigger and brighter varieties, and it is now one of the standard summer flowers, particularly in the warmer sections of the country.

The zinnia was named in honor of a German scientist, Professor Johann Gottfried Zinn, who died in 1759 at the early age of thirty-two. Before his death, he had won the respect of his fellow-scientists by publishing a book on the brain and the eye and an important botanical textbook.

In the language of flowers, the zinnia stands for thoughts of absent friends, and with this thought we leave our readers.

About the Author

Peter Limburg was graduated from Yale University and earned an MA in U.S. history at Columbia University. He has always been fascinated by word origins and has written two other books on the subject, *What's in the Names of Fruits?* and *What's in the Names of Antique Weapons?*

Mr. Limburg's hobbies include gardening, hiking, fishing, and nature study. He and his wife, Margareta, and their four children make their home in Bedford, New York.

About the Artist

Since being graduated from Pratt Institute, Heidi Palmer has illustrated *Getting to Know the Connecticut River* and *Nelly Custis' Diary* for Coward, McCann and Geoghegan. She likes traveling in the United States and Europe, enjoys farming, and lives in Montreal, Canada.